HEAT AND COMBUSTION

Grolier Educational
SHERMAN TURNPIKE, DANBURY, CONNECTICUT 06816

First published in the United States in 1998
by Grolier Educational, Sherman Turnpike,
Danbury, CT 06816

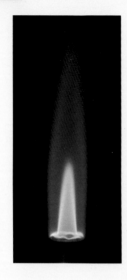

Author
Brian Knapp, BSc, PhD
Project consultant
*Keith B. Walshaw, MA, BSc, DPhil
(Head of Chemistry, Leighton Park School)*
Project Director
Duncan McCrae, BSc
Editor
Mary Sanders, BSc
Special photography
Ian Gledhill
Illustrations
The Ascenders Partnership, David Woodroffe
Electronic page makeup
The Ascenders Partnership
Designed and produced by
EARTHSCAPE EDITIONS
Print consultants
Chromo Litho Ltd
Reproduced in Malaysia by
Global Colour
Printed and bound in Italy by
L.E.G.O. SpA

Library of Congress Cataloging-in-Publication Data
ChemLab
    p. cm.
    Includes indexes.
    Contents: v.1.Gases, liquids, and solids –
v.2.Elements, compounds, and mixtures – v.3.The
periodic table – v.4.Metals – v.5.Acids, bases, and salts
– v.6.Heat and combustion – v.7.Oxidation and
reduction – v.8.Air and water chemistry – v.9.Carbon
chemistry – v.10.Energy and chemical change –
v.11.Preparations – v.12. Tests.
ISBN 0–7172–9146–4 (set). – ISBN 0–7172–9152–9 (v.6).
    1. Chemistry – Juvenile literature. [1. Chemistry.]
I. Grolier Educational (Firm)
QD35.C52 1997
540–dc21   97–23250
                                                       CIP
                                                        AC

Picture credits
All photographs are from the **Earthscape
Editions** photolibrary except the following:
(c=center t=top b=bottom l=left r=right)
Mary Evans Picture Library 7tl, 8cl, 9tr

*This product is manufactured from sustainable
managed forests. For every tree cut down at least
one more is planted.*

Contents

HOW TO USE THIS BOOK

These two pages show you how to get the most from this book.

❶ THE CONTENTS

Use the table of contents to see how this book is divided into themes. Each theme may have one or more demonstrations.

❷ THEMES

Each theme begins with a theory section on yellow-colored paper. Major themes may contain several pages of theory for the demonstrations that are presented on the subsequent pages. They also contain biographies of scientists whose work was important in the understanding of the theme.

❸ DEMONSTRATIONS

Demonstrations are at the heart of any chemistry study. However, many demonstrations cannot easily be shown to a whole class for health and safety reasons, because the demonstration requires a closeup view, because it is over too quickly, takes too long to complete, or because it requires special apparatus. The demonstrations shown here have been photographed especially to overcome these problems and give you a very closeup view of the key stages in each reaction.

The text, pictures, and diagrams are closely connected. To get the best from the demonstration, look closely at each picture as soon as its reference occurs in the text.

Many of the pictures show enlarged views of parts of the demonstration to help you see exactly what is happening. Notice, too, that most pictures form part of a sequence. You will find that it pays to look at the picture sequence more than once, and always be careful to make sure you can see exactly what is described in any picture before you move on.

The main heading for a demonstration or a set of demonstrations.

An introduction expands on the heading, summarizing the demonstration or group of demonstrations and their context in the theme.

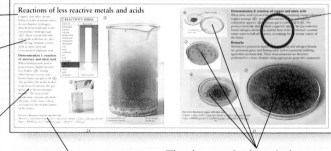

Each demonstration is carefully explained and illustrated with photographs and, where necessary, with diagrams, tables, and graphs. The illustrations referred to are numbered ①, ②, ③, etc.

Chemical equations are shown where appropriate (see the explanation of equations at the bottom of page 5).

The photographs show the key stages that you might see if witnessing a demonstration firsthand. Examine them very carefully against the text description.

APPARATUS

The demonstrations have been carefully conducted as representative examples of the main chemical processes. The apparatus used is standard; but other choices are possible, and you may see different equipment in your laboratory. So make sure you understand the principles behind the apparatus selected. The key pieces of apparatus are defined in the glossary.

❹ GLOSSARY OF TECHNICAL TERMS

Words with which you may be unfamiliar are shown in small capitals where they first occur in the text. Use the glossary on pages 66–74 to find more information about these technical words. Over four hundred items are presented alphabetically.

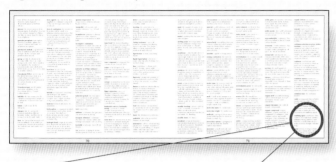

oxidizing agent: a substance that removes electrons from another substance being oxidized (and therefore is itself reduced) in a redox reaction. *Example:* chlorine (Cl$_2$).

❺ INDEX TO ALL VOLUMES IN THE SET

To look for key words in any of the 12 volumes that make up the ChemLab set, use the Master Index on pages 75 to 80. The instructions on page 75 show you how to cross-reference between volumes.

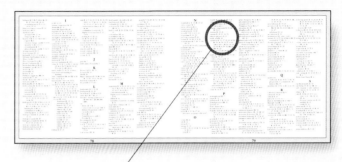

The most important locations of the term "oxidizing agent" are given in a master index that includes references to all of the volumes in the ChemLab set.

ABBREVIATIONS

Units are in the international metric system. Some units of measurement are abbreviated, or shortened, as follows:
°C = degrees Celsius
km = kilometer
m = meter
cm = centimeter
mm = millimeter
sq m = square meter
g = gram
kg = kilogram
kJ = kilojoule
l = liter

❻ CHEMICAL EQUATIONS

Important or relevant chemical equations are shown in written and symbolic form along with additional information.

What the reaction equation illustrates

Where relevant, the oxidation state is shown as Roman numerals in parentheses.

Word equation

Symbol equation
The symbols for each element can be found in any Periodic Table.

EQUATION: Reaction of copper and nitric acid

Copper + nitric acid ⇨ copper(II) nitrate + water + nitrogen dioxide

Cu(*s*) + 4HNO$_3$(*conc*) ⇨ Cu(NO$_3$)$_2$(*aq*) + 2H$_2$O(*l*) + 2NO$_2$(*g*)

Blue

The symbol indicating the state of each substance is shown as follows:
(*s*) = solid
(*g*) = gaseous
(*l*) = liquid
(*aq*) = aqueous
(*conc*) = concentrated

The two halves of the chemical equation are separated by the arrow that shows the progression of the reaction. Each side of the equation must balance.

Sometimes additional descriptions are given below the symbol equation.

The correct number of atoms, ions, and molecules and their proportions in any compound are shown by the numbers. A free electron is shown as an e⁻.

HEAT

HEAT is all around us. It is the form of energy that is involved when any kind of work is done.

For example, heat is released when two sticks are rubbed together or in a nuclear explosion. Heat can also be produced in a chemical reaction. Burning wood in a fire, for example, is a chemical reaction that produces heat, and our body produces heat as it digests the food we eat using chemical reactions.

(Above) Heating a substance need not necessarily result in any chemical change. It may simply change the temperature of the substance. The laboratory ceramic crucible and pipe-clay triangle shown in this picture are both being heated to a temperature in excess of 500°C. Despite the high temperature, they remain chemically unaltered, but instead, they have increased in temperature, emitting a strong glow.

Heating a substance adds energy and may cause a change. This change may be physical, such as a change in the volume, pressure, or density of the substance. However, the change may be chemical, for example, resulting in a COMPOUND breaking down into its component ELEMENTS. Elements may even combine to form new compounds.

COMBUSTION occurs when a gaseous substance reacts with a reactive gas such as oxygen to release heat and light. The VAPORS from coal and wood, for example, combust.

Developing a theory of heat

The first scientists to study the phenomenon of heat, such as Robert Boyle and Robert Hooke in the 17th century, deduced that heat is the outcome of the movement of particles within a substance. The TEMPERATURE of a substance was thought of as the intensity of the movement of these particles and therefore as a measure of the intensity of the heat produced.

In the 18th century Joseph Black noted that the amount of heat required to raise the temperature of a unit mass of a substance through one degree is nearly constant. He referred to this as HEAT CAPACITY. He also found that when ice melts, heat is absorbed without a change of temperature. This hidden heat is known as LATENT HEAT. Joseph Black also showed that when latent heat is absorbed or given out, the substance changes STATE between solid, liquid, or gas. This change of state is called a PHASE CHANGE.

GREAT EXPERIMENTAL SCIENTISTS

Robert Boyle

Robert Boyle (1627–1691) who, along with Lavoisier, is considered to be the father of chemistry, was born at Lismore Castle, Munster, Ireland.

In 1654 Boyle moved to Oxford, where he set up a small laboratory in his lodgings and later employed Robert Hooke as his assistant. Here, in 1662, Boyle invented the vacuum pump and did the experiments that allowed him to formulate BOYLE'S LAW, which relates the temperature of a fixed mass of gas to volume and pressure.

In 1668 Boyle moved to London and became a well-known society figure. He was a friend of Sir Isaac Newton and Samuel Pepys. He lived in London until his death on Dec. 30, 1691.

In 1660 (just 6 years before the Great Fire of London!) Boyle and Hooke studied combustion and, using an air pump, showed that charcoal and sulfur only catch fire when in the presence of air. They then showed that a mixture of either charcoal or sulfur and saltpeter catches fire when heated in the absence of air, so that the saltpeter and the air must contain some common substance (later found to be oxygen). He also studied the way in which certain organisms give out light, showing that they, too, needed air to emit light, and he compared them with glowing coal. By 1680 Boyle had discovered that by coating coarse paper with phosphorus, a flame was produced when a sulfur-tipped splint was drawn through the folded paper. Thus Boyle also invented the first match.

Boyle suggested the existence of simple atoms (which he called corpuscles) and that all phenomena could be explained in terms of the motion, shape, and position of these imperceptible corpuscles.

In the 19th century a mechanical theory of heat was deduced by Sir Humphry Davy. Much of the experimental work needed to support this theory was provided by James Prescott Joule. Joule showed that the heat produced from a system is directly proportional to the work done, in other words, that heat is simply a form of energy.

The unit of heat energy is now called the joule (J) in honor of the man most responsible for developing the theory of heat energy. However, the joule is a very small amount for use in most chemistry experiments, and so kilojoules (kJ) are often used.

Heat and physical change

When heat is added to, or taken away from, a substance, this must, in some way, be reflected in a change in that substance. For example, when a material is heated, it may swell (expand); and as it cools, it shrinks (contracts). This is seen most readily in gases, where expansion and contraction can be dramatic; but it also takes places in liquids and solids. This is a purely physical change – no chemical reactions have occurred.

There are other physical effects of heat changes. The material may melt, boil, or SUBLIME, i.e., undergo a change of state (a phase change) without any chemical change. For example, at certain critical temperatures substances change phase so dramatically that their whole molecular structure alters. Thus when enough heat energy is added to a solid, the particles of the solid break the BONDS holding them in a rigid

LATTICE and begin to move relatively freely. When this happens, a liquid forms. Similar phase changes are boiling, when a liquid changes to a gas, and sublimation, when a solid changes directly to a gas without going through the liquid phase.

Demonstrations relating to physical changes are shown on pages 10 to 17.

GREAT EXPERIMENTAL SCIENTISTS
Joseph Black

Joseph Black (1728–1799) was a Scottish chemist who was responsible for defining specific heat and discovering latent heat. He is thought of as one of the founders of modern chemistry.

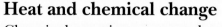

Black was born in Bordeaux, France, but he then went to live with relatives in Belfast, Ireland. Later he went to Glasgow and then Edinburgh, Scotland.

Black first became a doctor, but his interest in experiments kept him studying at the university. He studied the effects of heat on a number of rocks such as limestone (calcium carbonate) and dolomite (magnesium carbonate). From these experiments he discovered the gas, carbon dioxide.

Later Black studied the time that it took for a source of heat to raise the temperature of a given quantity of water to its boiling point and the time that it then took the same source of heat to vaporize the water. This is how he discovered latent heat and specific heat.

Heat and chemical change

Chemical reactions occur when bonds between ATOMS, MOLECULES, or IONS break and new ones form, the final arrangement of the particles being different from that in which they started.

Many types of reaction are possible. For example, a substance may break up into two simpler substances that then recombine to form the original compound on cooling. This is a reversible chemical reaction that involves a process known as DISSOCIATION.

Heat may also cause a compound to DECOMPOSE, that is, to break down into other chemicals that do not re-form the original one. This is called THERMAL DECOMPOSITION.

A MIXTURE of substances heated together may undergo a chemical reaction to yield new products.

If one or more of the REACTANTS is a gas and heat is given out once the reaction has started, the reaction is known as combustion (burning). Only if both reactants are gases in such an EXOTHERMIC reaction can a flame be seen.

Demonstrations relating to chemical changes are shown on pages 18 to 31, those relating to combustion on pages 36 to 64.

Measuring the heat changes in a chemical reaction

Almost all chemical reactions either emit heat to their surroundings (which is called an EXOTHERMIC reaction) or absorb heat from their surroundings (known as an ENDOTHERMIC reaction). For example,

is added to water, heat is given
hloride is dissolved in water,

xothermic and endothermic
ges 26 to 33.

enerated by any chemical
ALORIMETER. This is an
h a reaction takes place
eat to its surroundings. A
rise or fall in temperature
formation the heat energy
e found. A demonstration
ages 34 to 35.

TAL SCIENTISTS

ess (1802–1850) was born in Switzerland
lived in Russia. He first became a doctor but grew more
interested in chemistry and geology and held posts in both
chemistry and mining geology. One of his students was later
to become the professor who taught Dmitri Mendeleev (who
invented the PERIODIC TABLE).

In the 1830s Hess worked on the nature of heat and
chemistry. This was the time when he discovered Hess's Law. It
states that the heat absorbed or generated in a chemical reaction
depends only on the starting materials and final products and not
on what happens inbetween. (We now know this as a special case
of the law of conservation of energy.) For example, carbon can
be burned directly to carbon dioxide, or the carbon can first be
converted to carbon monoxide, and the carbon monoxide can
then be burned to carbon dioxide. The amount of heat given off
is the same in both cases. This amount of heat is the HEAT OF
COMBUSTION of carbon.

Hess's law is used to predict heat changes of reactions that are
difficult to perform directly.

GREAT EXPERIMENTAL SCIENTISTS
Robert Wilhelm Bunsen

Robert Wilhelm Bunsen (1811–
1899) was a German chemist
who invented the laboratory
burner that bears his name.
In 1841 he invented the Bunsen
electric cell to produce a very
bright arc light. He also used
his cell in ELECTROLYSIS,
obtaining metallic magnesium,
and he showed that magnesium
burns in air with an intense
light. In 1843, after years of
studying highly FLAMMABLE
and unpleasant arsenic-based
compounds, he lost his right
eye in an explosion and nearly
died of arsenic poisoning. Later
he became Professor of
Chemistry at Heidelberg.

Bunsen was particularly interested in heating metal compounds
in a flame until they became INCANDESCENT (gave off light).

In 1860 Bunsen, together with Gustav Kirchhoff, stated that
every chemical element was characterized by a particular
SPECTRUM (pattern of light waves). This meant that it should be
possible to identify elements in a compound by means of the light
rays they emit. This technique is called spectroscopy. Within a year
of beginning such spectroscopy, two new elements, rubidium and
cesium had been discovered.

To get a hot flame that burned evenly for these experiments,
Bunsen and his technician, Peter Desdega, designed the now
famous Bunsen burner.

Heat and physical change

The demonstrations on the next 8 pages illustrate heat and physical change.

Demonstration 1: phase changes of sulfur

When heat is applied to a substance, it changes state between solid, liquid, and gas, as shown by the demonstration on the next 4 pages. Each of these phase changes is accompanied by a change in the properties of the substance, as can be illustrated by the case of sulfur.

Sulfur is usually found in a laboratory as a crumbly yellow powder. If some sulfur powder is placed in a boiling tube and heated with a Bunsen flame (①), the powder reaches its melting point, and then it changes phase from a solid to an amber liquid. The reason for this is that solid sulfur atoms are arranged in "buckled" rings (②), each containing eight atoms. The energy of heating allows the rings to spread far enough apart to slide over one another.

Sulfur melts at 115°C. Despite this low melting temperature, it takes a long time for all of the sulfur to melt because sulfur is a poor conductor of heat.

When more heat is applied, the sulfur darkens, and the liquid becomes more VISCOUS (③). When it reaches 187°C, the viscosity has increased so much that the tube can be turned upside down, and the liquid will not move (④). The extra heating has ruptured the rings, and they have formed into chains that are now entangled.

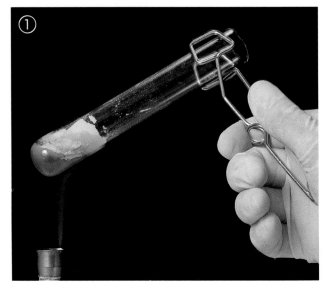

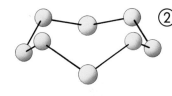

(Below and right) The "buckled" ring structure of a molecule of one form of sulfur, as seen from the side and above.

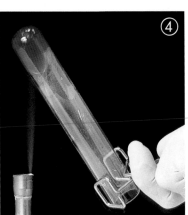

10

Heating it even further (to 444°C) makes the sulfur turn black. The liquid becomes mobile again because it has reached its BOILING POINT. The extra heat energy has ruptured the chains, and they now lie in short lengths that can easily move around. Some sulfur vapor is also given off.

The liquid can now be poured into cold water (⑤) so that it cools quickly. This process is known as crash-cooling. When the sulfur is picked out of the water, it can be pulled around like plastic (⑥) and drawn out into strings.

The crash-cooling has taken energy away quickly, causing the sulfur to form enormously long chains (⑦). As it is molded, it regains some energy and returns to the ring structure, gradually turning back to a solid. It will not return to a powder unless it is ground up.

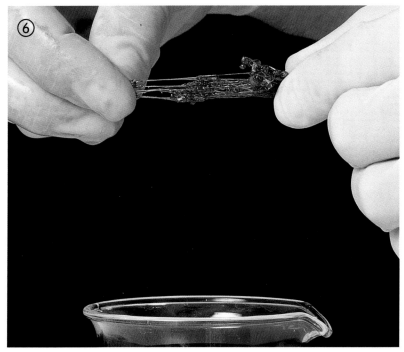

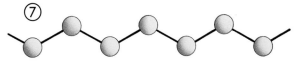

(Right) **Part of a chain of "plastic" sulfur.**

Demonstration 2: phase changes of camphor

Camphor is an example of a substance that can either melt then boil or sublime, depending on the rate of heating.

If crystals of camphor are placed on a watch glass and heated slowly over a water bath (⑧ & ⑨), they form into a "raft" that can be pushed around on the watch glass (⑩). The gentle heating has caused some of the substance to sublime. However, the vapor does not go far and sublimes back to a solid again on the upper edges of the crystals, which are away from the heat of the watch glass.

If, on the other hand, camphor crystals are heated strongly and rapidly enough in a boiling tube, the camphor can be made to melt (⑪). Then it almost immediately boils, producing two changes of state, while a white deposit forms in the middle of the tube. Thus on vigorous heating in a boiling tube some of the solid changes into vapor and sublimes, as it did when heated slowly on a watch glass. However, because the

⑨

Camphor

⑧

Spatula with camphor

Beaker filled with water to make a water bath and placed on a gauze pad

Watch glass

Bunsen burner

camphor was being heated rapidly, it continued to get hotter even though it was subliming, and this allowed the remainder of the camphor both to melt and boil, creating a vapor.

Where the vapor met the cold tube, it immediately sublimed to solid and produced the opaque small crystals that make the white deposit on the middle of the tube (⑫).

Remarks

During strong heating with a Bunsen flame the camphor vapor may combine with oxygen from the air and ignite to produce a flame in the upper end of the boiling tube.

Chemical change is distinct from physical change. In this case the physical changes in the bottom of the tube are the changes of state, whereas the flame is an example of combustion, a chemical change. (See also page 42.)

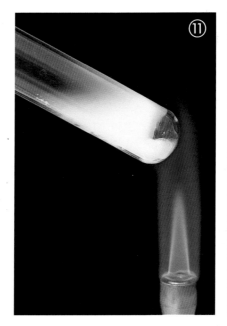

Pushing raft of crystals

⑩

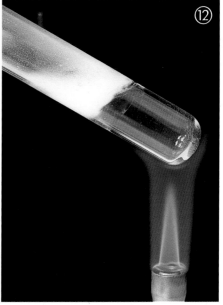

⑪

⑫

Demonstration 3: sublimation of iodine

When iodine is heated strongly in a small test tube, it will melt. When it is heated gently in a large flask, it changes directly from a solid to a vapor.

In this demonstration solid iodine crystals are scattered on the bottom of a flat-bottomed flask (⑬). A watch glass, rather than a stopper, is placed on top of the flask to prevent loss of too much vapor, but at the same time allowing the gas to expand on heating.

Because iodine vapor is poisonous, the demonstration is performed in a fume chamber.

Shortly after being heated, a purple vapor appears in the flask as the iodine crystals sublime (⑭). The density of the purple vapor increases, and at the same time, purple crystals begin to grow on the upper (cooler) parts of the flask (away from the heated base). These are also crystals of iodine.

Remarks

The growth of crystals on the upper part of the flask depends on the heating conditions in the flask. Moderate heating produces large crystals. When the iodine is heated more strongly, a very large amount of iodine is available to sublime, and many small crystals are able to form. Because there is now competition between the crystals for the iodine vapor, many grow but only to a modest size.

⑬ Iodine pellets

⑭ Watch glass

Demonstration 4: heat changes during melting

Pure substances have fixed physical properties. This means, for example, that a pure substance will always melt and boil at the same temperature (at a fixed pressure).

The melting point is the temperature at which a solid turns into a liquid or a liquid solidifies. Because it is difficult to get a thermometer into a solid substance, it is far more convenient to melt the substance, put a stirring thermometer into the liquid, and then measure the temperature as it solidifies (⑮).

In fact, measuring the temperature is not as difficult as might at first be thought for two reasons. It is easy to spot the first crystals that form in the liquid as it begins to solidify, and also, the temperature stops dropping for a while during solidification as the liquid turns into the solid phase and releases energy in the form of latent heat.

An alternative method that doesn't rely on the chance spotting of crystals is to plot a graph of temperature against time and look for the break in the curve (noted by a horizontal segment) corresponding to the release of latent heat (⑯). In this case the temperature recorded on the thermometer is read every half minute until the substance has solidified, and a graph is plotted of temperature against time (⑰).

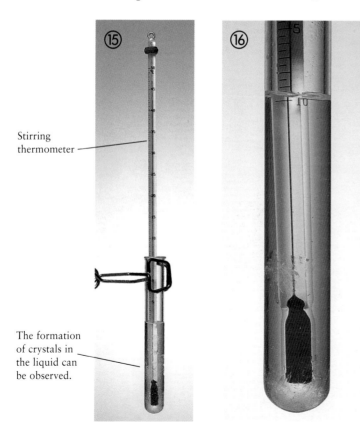

Stirring thermometer

The formation of crystals in the liquid can be observed.

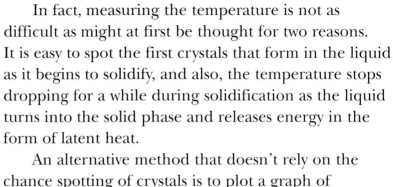

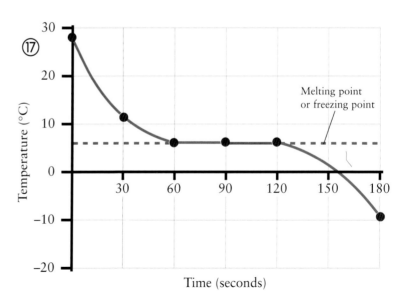

(Above) The temperature falls and then remains constant at the freezing point of the liquid, while it freezes to its solid form.

Demonstration 5: solubility and temperature

The amount of a substance that will dissolve in a given amount of a SOLVENT varies strongly with temperature.

To investigate changes in SOLUBILITY with temperature, 5 g of potassium chlorate ($KClO_3$) are weighed out into a boiling tube (⑱ & ⑲). Next, 10 cm³ of distilled water are added (⑳), and the mixture heated over a Bunsen flame while being stirred with a stirring thermometer.

When all of the solid has dissolved (㉑), the tube is allowed to cool, but the stirring is continued. The temperature of the solution is recorded when the first crystals appear (㉒). At this stage almost all of the potassium chlorate is still dissolved, and the solution is saturated. Therefore, at this temperature 10 cm³ of water dissolves 5 g of potassium chlorate.

Another 5 cm³ of water can now be added, the solution heated, then allowed to cool, and the recording sequence repeated as before (㉓). This time when the first crystals appear, the temperature is found to be lower than before. The demonstration is continued, adding the same additional quantity of water, reheating and cooling until crystals appear each time.

To see the changes in solubility, a graph is drawn based on the tabulated results.

Remarks

Solubility can be expressed as g of a SOLUTE per 100 g of solvent, i.e., 5 g in 10 cm³ (10 g) is 50 g in 100 g or a solubility of 50. This is used in calculating the solubility for the graph.

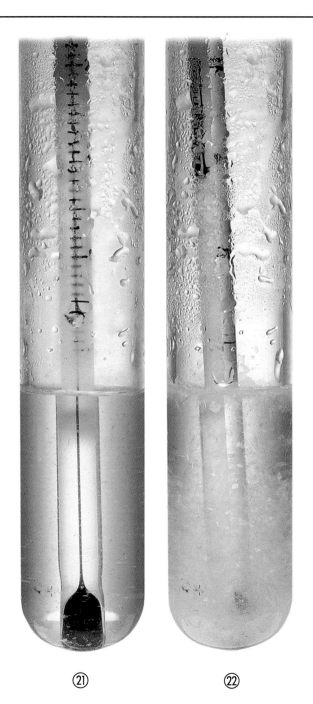

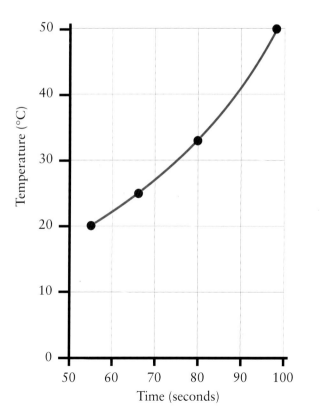

㉑   ㉒   ㉓

DATA FOR CHART
Solubility of potassium chlorate:
mass of solute 5 g to which additional
amounts of water are added as solvent.

Volume of solvent (cm³)	Solubility (g/100 g)	Temperature (°C)
10	50	98
15	33	80
20	25	66
25	20	56

Heat and chemical change

Heating a substance to cause chemical change is a very common procedure in chemistry. A wide variety of responses can be produced, as is illustrated by the following demonstrations.

CHEMICAL EFFECTS OF HEAT

Heat and chemical reactions interact in four ways:

1. A chemical reaction may need a continuous supply of heat energy to work at all.
2. A chemical reaction may need an external source of heat energy to begin, but once under way, the reaction may then give out at least enough heat to sustain itself.
3. A chemical reaction may give out heat to its surroundings without any external source of heating involved.
4. A chemical reaction may draw in heat from its surroundings even at low temperatures.

Each of these interactions will be shown in the demonstrations that follow.

Demonstration 1: chemical changes with limewater

Blowing into cold limewater (calcium hydroxide) creates a precipitate of calcium carbonate (①). The carbon dioxide in the breath reacts with the limewater. Continued blowing makes the solution turn clear again because the additional amount of carbon dioxide reacts with the calcium carbonate to produce soluble and colorless calcium bicarbonate (calcium hydrogen carbonate).

Heating the colorless solution (②) will turn the solution cloudy again because calcium bicarbonate is not stable in hot water, and the bicarbonate changes back to calcium carbonate, which is insoluble.

EQUATION: Calcium carbonate to calcium bicarbonate
Calcium carbonate + water + carbon dioxide ➩ *calcium bicarbonate*
$CaCO_3(s) + H_2O(l) + CO_2(g)$ ➩ $Ca(HCO_3)_2(aq)$

EQUATION: Change from calcium bicarbonate solution to calcium carbonate
Calcium bicarbonate solution ➩ *calcium carbonate + carbon dioxide + water*
$Ca(HCO_3)_2(aq)$ ➩ $CaCO_3(s) + CO_2(g) + H_2O(l)$
With heat

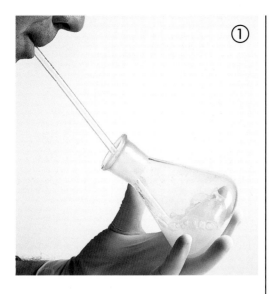

Demonstration 2: heating can drive off WATER OF CRYSTALLIZATION

Some substances can exist with varying amounts of water. A solid that contains water is referred to as HYDRATED. In this demonstration some hydrated crystals of sodium carbonate decahydrate ($Na_2CO_3 \cdot 10H_2O$) (③) are heated in a boiling tube (④). The crystals first melt, then the liquid boils. and the water is given off as steam (⑤). The water being released can be tested for, using blue cobalt chloride crystals that are turned pink by water.

The white powder that remains when the steam stops being evolved is ANHYDROUS sodium carbonate (Na_2CO_3) (⑥). It contains no water.

EQUATION: Heating hydrated sodium carbonate

Sodium carbonate decahydrate ⇨ sodium carbonate + water (steam)

$$Na_2CO_3 \cdot 10H_2O(s) \Rightarrow Na_2CO_3(s) + 10H_2O(g)$$

Heat given out

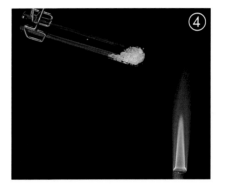

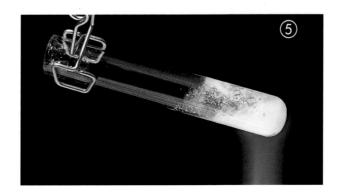

Demonstration 3: decomposing mercury(II) oxide

Mercury is so far down the REACTIVITY SERIES that mercury(II) oxide (HgO) is easily decomposed into the metal and oxygen by heating.

If red mercury(II) oxide is heated in a boiling tube (⑦), within a few minutes the powder turns black and begins to decompose into mercury and oxygen gas (⑧).

The mercury evaporates and condenses onto the colder region near the mouth of the tube, where it re-forms as a mercury mirror (⑨).

(Below) Effect of heat on metal oxides

Metal oxide	Action of heat
Potassium oxide	
Sodium oxide	
Calcium oxide	
Magnesium oxide	Not decomposed even at very high temperatures.
Zinc oxide	
Iron oxide	
Lead oxide	
Copper oxide	
Silver oxide	
Mercury oxide	Decomposed on heating into the metal and releasing oxygen.

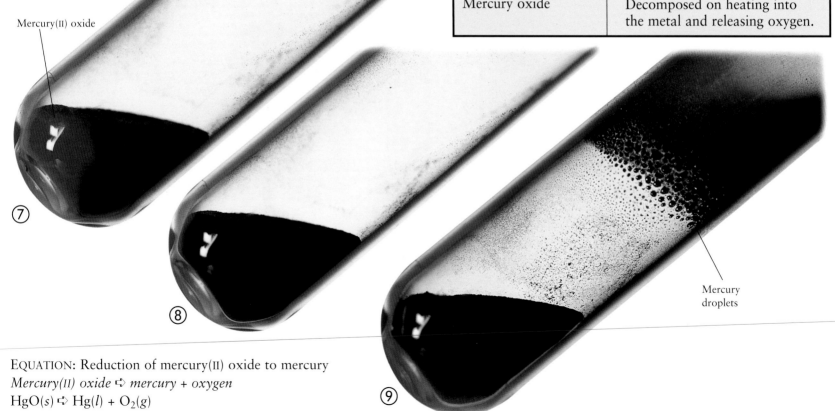

Mercury(II) oxide

⑦

⑧

⑨

Mercury droplets

EQUATION: Reduction of mercury(II) oxide to mercury
Mercury(II) oxide ⇨ mercury + oxygen
$HgO(s) \Rightarrow Hg(l) + O_2(g)$

Demonstration 4: decomposing potassium nitrate

Potassium is a very reactive metal, and its compounds are not easily decomposed. Thus heating only releases some of the oxygen in the compound.

When potassium nitrate (KNO_3) is melted (⑩), it produces a greenish-yellow liquid (potassium nitrite) (⑪) and gives off oxygen gas. Potassium nitrite is not decomposed by heating; and when the heat is removed, it eventually cools to a white solid.

The presence of oxygen is revealed by the rekindling (combustion) of a glowing splint (⑫ & ⑬, on page 22).

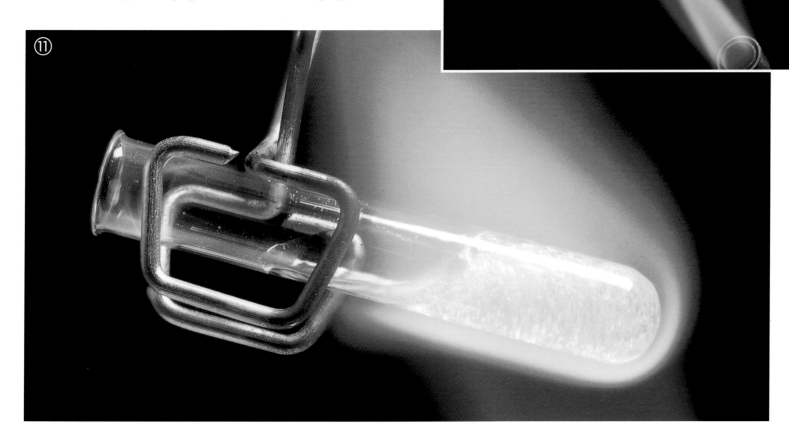

EQUATION: Decomposing potassium nitrate with heat
Potassium nitrate ⇨ *potassium nitrite + oxygen*
$2KNO_3(s) \Rightarrow 2KNO_2(s) + O_2(g)$

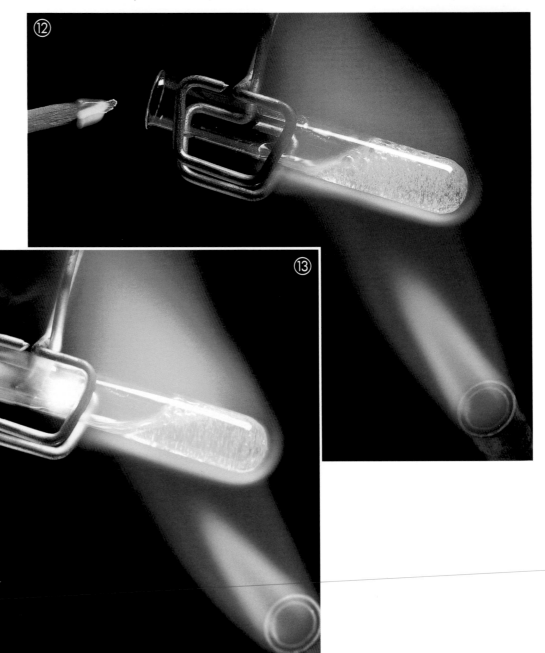

Demonstration 5: decomposing lead(II) nitrate

Lead is not a very reactive metal. As a result, its compounds are not very stable, and they decompose easily.

When lead(II) nitrate ($PbNO_3$), which is a white powder (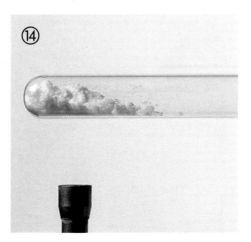), is heated in a boiling tube, it changes to a yellow color as it melts, and brown nitrogen dioxide gas is released (⑮), which mixes with the oxygen also being released. Further strong heating then makes it decompose to lead oxide. The lead oxide usually fuses into the glass of the boiling tube at this stage.

In this case adding heat energy allows the nitrate to decompose. Some of the energy used in the process can be heard as the crystals of lead nitrate break up, a process called DECREPITATION.

Decomposition releases brown nitrogen dioxide gas and oxygen gas.

EQUATION: Decomposition of lead(II) nitrate
Lead(II) nitrate ⇨ lead monoxide + nitrogen dioxide + oxygen
$$2Pb(NO_3)_2(s) \Rightarrow 2PbO(s) + 4NO_2(g) + O_2(g)$$

(*Below*) Effect of heat on metal nitrates

Metal nitrate	Action of heat
Potassium nitrate	When heated to a high temperature, oxygen is released. A nitrite remains, and no nitrogen dioxide is produced.
Sodium nitrate	
Calcium nitrate	Decomposed on heating to produce the metal oxide, nitrogen dioxide, and oxygen.
Magnesium nitrate	
Zinc nitrate	
Iron nitrate	
Lead nitrate	
Copper nitrate	
Silver nitrate	Decomposed, producing the metal, oxygen, and nitrogen dioxide.
Mercury nitrate	Unstable. Does not exist at room temperature.

⑮

⑭

Demonstration 6: decomposing calcium carbonate

Calcium is a very reactive element, and its compounds are quite stable except at very high temperatures. Calcium carbonate, for example, only decomposes at furnace temperatures.

The apparatus shows how calcium carbonate can be decomposed into calcium oxide in the laboratory. It consists of an iron cylinder (the kiln) containing a tray on which the limestone rests (⑯).

A cover is put over the kiln to help conserve the heat and to allow the temperature inside the kiln to rise as high as possible.

The limestone is now heated using as intense a Bunsen flame as can be achieved (⑰). It usually requires three or more burners to produce sufficient heating. The temperature that has to be achieved is about 1500°C.

As the limestone becomes hot, it begins to glow and break down. In the picture you can see the limestone glowing a yellow-red color (⑱). Over the space of about 10 minutes the limestone decomposes to form a white solid, calcium oxide, and gives off carbon dioxide gas (⑲).

⑱

(Below) Effect of heat on metal carbonates

Metal carbonate	Action of heat
Potassium carbonate	Not decomposed even at very high temperatures.
Sodium carbonate	
Calcium carbonate	Decomposed on heating into the metal oxide and releasing carbon dioxide. The ease of decomposition increases as you move down the list.
Magnesium carbonate	
Zinc carbonate	
Iron carbonate	
Lead carbonate	
Copper carbonate	Unstable – does not exist at room temperature.
Silver carbonate	

EQUATION: Calcium carbonate decomposes
Calcium carbonate ⇨ calcium oxide + carbon dioxide
$CaCO_3(s) ⇨ CaO(s) + CO_2(g)$

⑲

Exothermic reactions

An exothermic reaction is one in which the energy needed for the products of the reaction is less than the energy contained within the REACTANTS. One of the most obvious examples of an exothermic reaction is combustion (see page 36).

If a reactant is used for its exothermic properties during the reaction, then the reactant is called a FUEL. However, in many chemical reactions the heat energy released is not the main objective. In fact, the majority of reactions are exothermic, although many give out too little heat for this to be obvious.

Demonstration 1: water and calcium oxide

This demonstration uses large pieces of calcium oxide placed on a watch glass. Water from a pipette is then dripped onto some of the blocks, while others are left unwetted as a control (①). As the blocks are made wet, steam is immediately produced that condenses on the pipette (②), while the blocks begin to swell and break down into a powder, calcium hydroxide (③ & ④). The steam is an indication of just how exothermic this reaction is.

EQUATION: The formation of calcium hydroxide
Calcium oxide + water ⇨ calcium hydroxide
$CaO(s) + H_2O(l) ⇨ Ca(OH)_2(aq)$
Heat given out

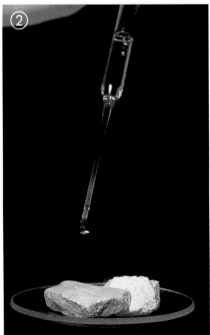
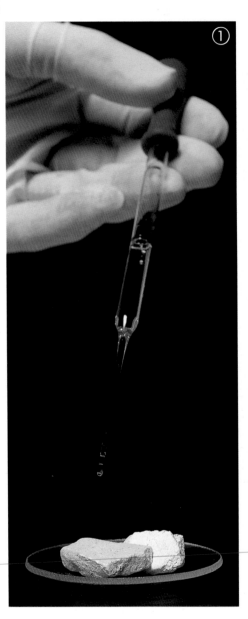
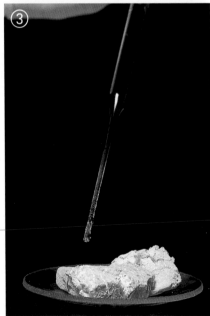

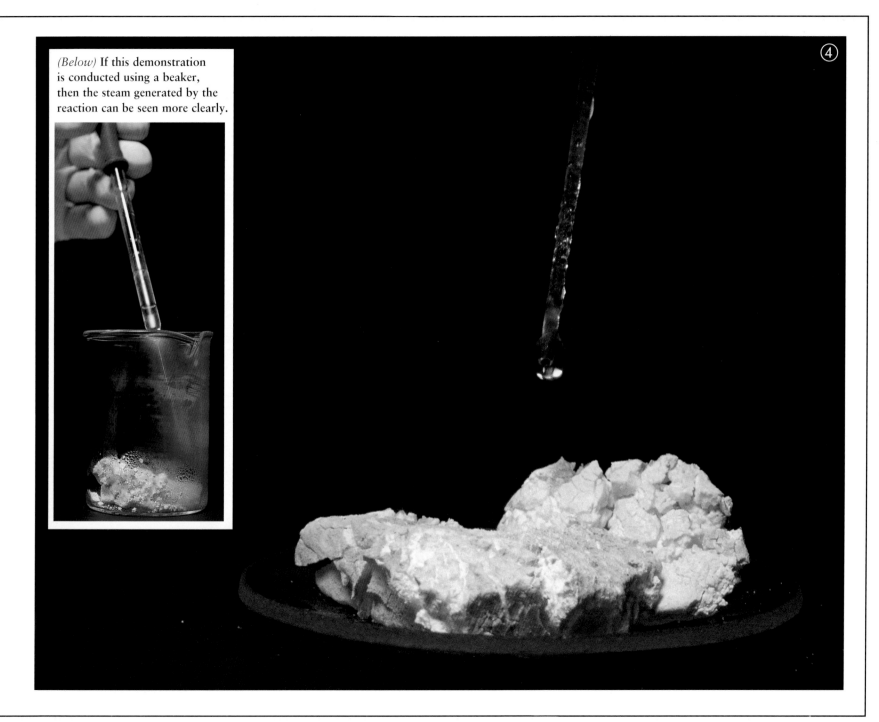

(Below) **If this demonstration is conducted using a beaker, then the steam generated by the reaction can be seen more clearly.**

④

Demonstration 2: sugar and concentrated sulfuric acid

Sugar (sucrose) is a carbohydrate, that is, a compound containing carbon, hydrogen, and oxygen. Concentrated sulfuric acid is a strong DEHYDRATING AGENT, and it reacts with the sugar to remove the hydrogen and oxygen as water, a process that is highly exothermic.

A small amount of white sugar is placed in the bottom of a beaker. Concentrated sulfuric acid is then poured onto the sugar (⑤). The sugar turns yellow (⑥), then dark brown (⑦). At the same time, bubbling is seen, as the considerable heat produced during the reaction causes the water from the glucose to turn into steam.

Within a minute or two the sugar has turned black (⑧). At this stage the glucose is a hot, syrupy liquid, which does not readily allow the steam to escape, so some of it remains trapped as bubbles, creating a foam. The black substance surrounding the bubbles is now carbon (⑨).

Remarks

The concentrated sulfuric acid acts as a dehydrating agent in this reaction, as is shown by the chemical equation.

As the steam is given off, bubbles form, which cause the carbon to develop into a volcano of a substance that, on cooling, has the feel of coke.

The concentrated sulfuric acid remains trapped in this cakelike mass.

⑦

⑥

⑤

⑧

⑨

EQUATION: Dehydration of sucrose
Sucrose + sulfuric acid ⇨ water + carbon + sulfuric acid
$C_{12}H_{22}O_{11}(s) + H_2SO_4(conc) \Rightarrow 11H_2O(g) + 12C(s) + H_2SO_4(aq)$
Heat given out

Demonstration 3: the heat in a fuel

One of the most common reactions associated with the release of heat is OXIDATION. Fuels, for example, are oxidized when they burn. This demonstration shows the violent reaction of a fuel (cyclohexanol) with concentrated nitric acid.

This demonstration is performed in a tall gas jar inside a fume chamber (⑩). A very small volume of (colorless) cyclohexanol is poured into one small measuring cylinder, and a small volume of (colorless) nitric acid into another cylinder.

The gas jar contains a thermometer that will show the temperature in the gas jar during the demonstration.

The cyclohexanol is poured into the tall gas jar (⑪), and the nitric acid added (⑫). The nitric acid

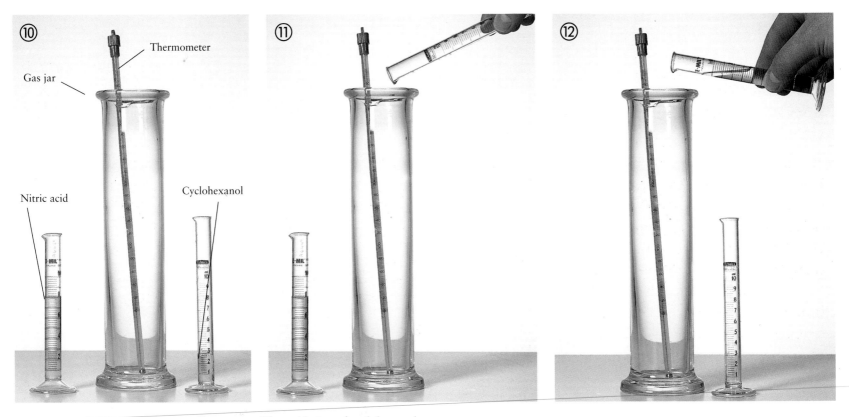

EQUATION: The oxidation of cyclohexanol

Cyclohexanol + concentrated nitric acid ⇨ nitrogen dioxide + adipic acid + water

$C_6H_{11}OH(l) + 8HNO_3(conc) \Rightarrow 8NO_2(g) + (CH_2)_4(CO_2H)_2(l) + 5H_2O(l)$

Heat given out

is added as quickly as possible because the reaction is almost instantaneous and is of such violence that the hands of the demonstrator need to be clear of the apparatus by the time the reaction starts.

The reaction immediately produces a "volcanic" eruption of bubbling liquid and a gush of brown nitrogen dioxide gas (⑬). As the bubbling subsides (⑭) and the gas clears (⑮), the temperature of the thermometer is found to have risen from 20°C before the reagents were added to 110°C within 5 seconds.

Remarks

It is very important to notice that only small volumes of starting reactants are being used here. Large amounts could produce a reaction of dangerously violent proportions.

The use of a fume chamber is important to remove any risk of droplets of nitric acid escaping as the reaction proceeds, and because nitrogen dioxide is poisonous.

Endothermic reactions

An endothermic reaction is one in which the energy required by the products is more than can be supplied by the reactants. As a result, heat is taken from the surroundings.

Demonstration: barium hydroxide octahydrate and ammonium nitrate

This demonstration will show an endothermic reaction in two ways: by measuring the fall of temperature within a reacting mixture, and by seeing how it makes water freeze.

The apparatus consists of a ceramic tile, a beaker and a thermometer. To show how the endothermic reaction takes heat from its surroundings, some drops of water are placed on the tile (①), and the beaker then placed on the tile and slid around until the water makes an even film between the tile and the beaker. The objective will be to freeze the tile to the beaker.

Barium hydroxide octahydrate is then ground into a fine powder using a PESTLE AND MORTAR and then placed in the beaker (②). A similarly ground down powder of ammonium nitrate is added to the beaker (③) and stirred briskly with a stirring thermometer (④), having first taken the value of the temperature (which in this case was 20°C).

As the two solids are mixed together, they begin to react and turn into a liquid. As this happens, the temperature falls dramatically (⑤). In this demonstration the stirring thermometer reading fell to −20°C within a minute, a 40°C fall in temperature.

The fall in temperature is so fast that it takes a few moments longer for the cold to penetrate the bottom of the beaker and to begin to freeze the water on the

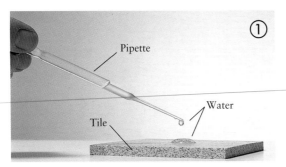

① Pipette / Water / Tile

② Stirring thermometer

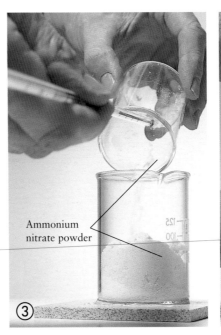

③ Barium hydroxide powder

Ammonium nitrate powder

④

tile. When this finally happens, the beaker and tile can be lifted completely clear of the laboratory bench (⑥)!

Remarks

This is actually a two-stage reaction. When mixed in a flask, the two solids, barium hydroxide octahydrate ($Ba(OH)_2 \cdot 8H_2O$) and ammonium nitrate (NH_4NO_3), undergo an acid-base reaction. The water produced by this reaction dissolves excess ammonium nitrate, and this second stage is actually the endothermic reaction.

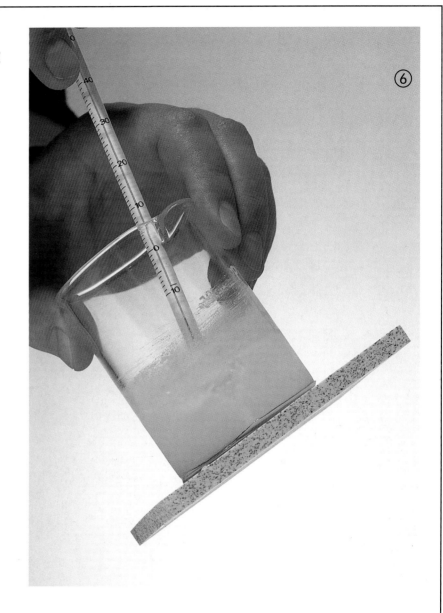

EQUATION: Endothermic reaction between barium hydroxide and ammonium nitrate

Barium hydroxide + ammonium nitrate ⇨ *barium nitrate + ammonium hydroxide + water*

$$Ba(OH)_2 \cdot 8H_2O(s) + 2NH_4NO_3(s) \Rightarrow Ba(NO_3)_2(aq) + 2NH_4OH(aq) + 8H_2O(l)$$

Heat taken in

Calorimetry

It is possible to determine the amount of heat produced or consumed in exothermic and endothermic reactions by using a calorimeter. This is a simple insulated device that records the temperature rise or fall.

Demonstration: relative reactivities of metals

In this demonstration the reaction of an acid and a number of metals will be used to determine the relative reactivities of the metals through the heat produced during the reaction.

A test tube is first weighed ((1)), then a small amount of magnesium added, and the tube and contents reweighed ((2)). Subtraction of the weights gives the mass of the magnesium used, which in this case was 0.57 g.

A simple calorimeter is made up of a plastic beaker inside an expanded polystyrene cup placed in a glass beaker. Expanded polystyrene has high insulating properties. The beaker acts as a support for the cup.

Sufficient dilute sulfuric acid is now poured into the cup to ensure that it is in excess and that all the magnesium will react ((3)). In this demonstration 20 cm^3 of 2 molar (2M) sulfuric acid are used (that is, the concentration of the acid is two moles in every thousand cm^3). A stirring thermometer is now placed in the acid to measure the starting temperature ((4)), which in this case was 20°C.

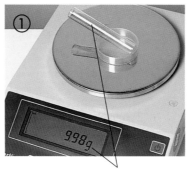

① Weight of empty test tube

② Weight of test tube with magnesium powder

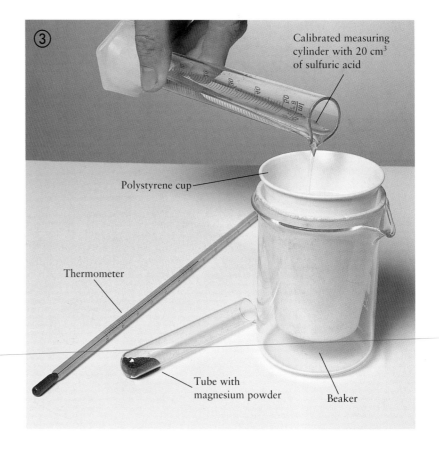

③ Calibrated measuring cylinder with 20 cm^3 of sulfuric acid

Polystyrene cup

Thermometer

Tube with magnesium powder

Beaker

The known weight of magnesium in the tube is now poured into the cup (⑤), and the stirring thermometer used to stir the contents of the tube, the thermometer being read frequently. This reaction is quite vigorous, and hydrogen is given off. The maximum temperature reached by the thermometer is now recorded, which in this case was 72°C.

The demonstration is then repeated using zinc powder instead of the magnesium powder. The reaction of the zinc and the acid release enough heat to give a highest temperature of 46°C.

Remarks

The insulated calorimeter allows the measurement of temperature rises in reactions that are only slightly exothermic. The constant conditions inside the calorimeter also allow comparative measurements to be made.

EQUATION: **Magnesium and sulfuric acid**
Magnesium + sulfuric acid ⇨ magnesium sulfate + hydrogen
$Mg(s) + H_2SO_4(aq) ⇨ MgSO_4(aq) + H_2(g)$
Heat given out

EQUATION: **Zinc and sulfuric acid**
Zinc + sulfuric acid ⇨ zinc sulfate + hydrogen
$Zn(s) + H_2SO_4(aq) ⇨ ZnSO_4(aq) + H_2(g)$
Heat given out

COMBUSTION

Combustion is a reaction in which an element or compound is oxidized to release energy. Some combustion reactions are slow, such as the combustion of the sugar we eat to provide our energy. If the combustion results in a flame, it is called burning (see page 44). Some combustion reactions produce light and heat but do not produce flames (see page 54 to 55).

A flame occurs where *gases* combust and release heat and light. At least two gases are therefore required if there is to be a flame.

A combustion reaction results in the original element or compound being oxidized. Given the presence of oxygen this will result in an OXIDE or oxides being produced. Since heat is released during combustion, the reaction is described as exothermic.

Fuels

Substances that undergo combustion are described as fuels. Because of the plentiful supply of oxygen in air and the uses for the energy produced, fuels and combustion reactions are valuable to us. For example, we use fuels such as gas and diesel oil to drive the engines of vehicles that transport us (see page 40). Many of our most important fuels, such as gas, diesel, kerosene, and natural gas, are derived from petroleum oil and are

mixtures of HYDROCARBONS. Another important fossil fuel is coal.

Substances that will not combust, and therefore cannot be used as fuels, include the noble gases, nitrogen gas, and substances that are themselves a product of combustion, such as some oxides, sulfides, and chlorides.

(Above) This hot air balloon uses propane gas as its fuel. The combustion of the propane produces sufficient heat to warm the air inside the balloon and lift it and its passengers off the ground. Propane is a hydrocarbon, and its combustion produces a bright flame. The gas is almost completely oxidized to water as steam and carbon dioxide.

The history of combustion

The excitement, usefulness, and danger of flames have meant that combustion, burning, and fuels have long been a subject of intense scientific study. Indeed, in the days of the alchemists flames were wrongly thought to be one of the four elements of matter.

The first careful studies of combustion were made in the 17th century by scientists such as Robert Boyle and Robert Hooke. They began to compare the weights and volume of the fuel to the products of combustion. By this means they were able to deduce that the products of burning contained the weight of another substance (later found to be oxygen) and to begin to understand the way in which matter was rapidly oxidized during a fire (see page 48).

In the 19th century other scientists, including Robert Bunsen, developed the understanding even further.

Oxidizing agents and combustion

Combustion occurs when a fuel reacts with an OXIDIZING AGENT. Most frequently we see combustion with oxygen, since it is plentiful in air. Other oxidizing agents include oxygen-rich compounds such as ammonium perchlorate (NH_4ClO_4), potassium permanganate ($KMnO_4$), hydrogen peroxide (H_2O_2), nitrogen dioxide (NO_2), and nitric acid (HNO_3).

However, oxidizing agents do not have to contain oxygen, and combustion occurs with the halogens, such as chlorine. In the demonstration to the left a wax taper is being held in the air above a sealed gas jar containing chlorine. The taper burns in the oxygen of the air with a yellow flame (①), releasing carbon dioxide gas and carbon as soot particles.

When the wax taper is put into a gas jar of chlorine, the taper still burns, this time with a red flame (②). It also liberates carbon particles (soot) and produces a steamy gas – in this case, harmful hydrogen

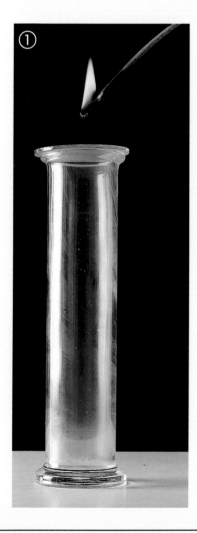

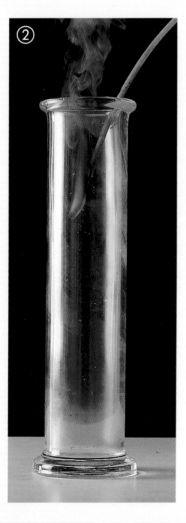

chloride. This shows that chlorine is a very effective oxidizing agent.

Some substances, such as nitrocellulose, contain atoms of both fuel and oxidizing agent within the same molecule. This is what makes them such good explosives.

Combustion temperatures

Each fuel burns with its own characteristic temperature. The highest temperature reached by burning a FOSSIL FUEL in air is about 1900°C. Oxyacetylene torches can reach temperatures of over 3300°C.

(Above) In oxyacetylene cutting and welding the acetylene fuel (kept liquefied in a cylinder) is fed into a nozzle, where it combines with oxygen supplied from a separate cylinder. When this mixture is ignited, the reaction releases a large amount of heat while producing carbon dioxide gas and water vapor.

Oxyacetylene torches can reach combustion temperatures of over 3300°C. This flame is so hot that it can melt metal, which is why it is used in welding.

The temperature to which a fuel must be raised before it begins to burn is called the IGNITION TEMPERATURE and varies among different substances. Paper, wood, and gas ignite at roughly 250°C, and coal at 500°C.

The flame

A flame can be seen as a cone of light in which a mixture of hot gases is burning. It surrounds a tapering column of a cool, unburned (fuel) gas.

In a candle the fuel is wax, and the wax is melted and vaporized from the end of the wick. Air is drawn toward the base of the flame so that the fuel is at the center of a ring; the air is drawn from around the outside of the ring toward the inside. Such a flame gives off considerable light because it contains incandescent soot (carbon) particles (see pages 42 and 44).

In a simple flame not all of the gas is mixed with the oxygen of the surrounding air during combustion, and some gas escapes unburned from the flame region.

A laboratory Bunsen burner (see pages 45 to 47) has a different type of flame. The fuel is in the form of a gas that can be mixed with air before it is burned (depending on the hole in the sleeve of the Bunsen burner). The flame from this mixture forms three zones. The innermost part of the flame consists of cold, unburned gas. The middle layer is very thin; it is in this layer that the fuel and the mixed air react. Any residual combustible gas burns as it mixes with the surrounding air to form the outermost layer of the flame. This outer cone is often difficult to see. The hottest part of the flame is just outside the tip of the inner cone (③).

Better combustion results in higher heat and less light with no carbon particles. This is why laboratory burners have a subdued blue flame (and a characteristic roaring sound) when the sleeve is turned to mix the air at the base of the burner, but why they have a bright yellow flame when the air ring is closed.

③

(Below) **A blue Bunsen flame**

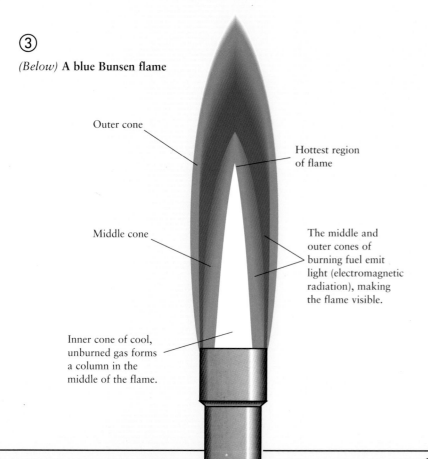

Outer cone

Hottest region of flame

Middle cone

The middle and outer cones of burning fuel emit light (electromagnetic radiation), making the flame visible.

Inner cone of cool, unburned gas forms a column in the middle of the flame.

Conditions for a flame

Two systems can provide the conditions for a flame during combustion. In one arrangement the fuel and the oxidizing agent are mixed before combustion begins. This happens, for example, in a Bunsen burner. Explosives have both fuel and oxidizing agent mixed in their molecular structures.

In the other system the fuel and the oxidizing agent are mixed as they burn. This happens as a candle or a coal fire burns. In these cases the vapor from the fuel diffuses into the air containing oxygen, and the flame zone occurs where the two mix.

Spontaneous combustion

In some circumstances a substance can ignite and combust on the heat generated within the substance. This is usually a consequence of rapid oxidation. The material may also vaporize and burst into flames. This can occur where oxygen is trapped within piles of materials such as straw in haystacks. In other cases the presence of an oxidizing agent close to a potential source of fuel in a dry mixture can also trap the heat, allowing temperatures to rise to the ignition point of the fuel. This is called SPONTANEOUS COMBUSTION (see page 64).

Preventing combustion

Because combustion is caused by the rapid oxidation of a material, most ways of controlling a fire involve two stages: (a) reducing the temperature, thus slowing down the rate of reaction, and (b) denying the fuel a further supply of oxidizing agent.

A simple fire blanket thrown over a fire helps starve a fire of the oxygen needed for continued burning. Remembering that most oxides do not burn, this provides a range of possible materials to prevent combustion. Water (hydrogen oxide) acts to reduce the temperature and also to cover the fuel so that very little air can reach it. Carbon dioxide gas covers the fire and thus keeps the oxygen out. Powder extinguishers are made of a noncombustible powder oxide that simply blankets the burning material and stops oxygen getting to the fuel.

A flame-retardant is a chemical used on clothing and furniture fabrics to prevent the material from burning easily. The most common chemicals are based on phosphoric or sulfuric acids. When the chemical begins to burn, the compound decomposes, leaving an acid behind that can react with the fabric and change it from a hydrocarbon fuel to carbon. The carbonized (charred) surface produces little fuel with which the oxygen in the air can react. The same chemical reaction releases carbon dioxide, again preventing oxygen from getting to the material. Borax (sodium borate, $Na_2B_4O_7 \bullet 10H_2O$) is another material sometimes used as a flame-retardant coating. Borax melts at fairly low temperatures, smothering the fabric and keeping oxygen from the inflammable fabric.

A problem with some flame-retarding materials is that they release toxic gases as they react, thereby making it necessary for firefighters to use breathing apparatus.

The internal combustion engine

One of the most widely used fuels is gasoline, a hydrocarbon liquid that ignites at 350°C with the oxygen in the surrounding air. The stages in the operation of a combustion engine are shown in the diagrams below and to the right.

The fuel is formed into a mist of tiny droplets (it is "atomized") and then sucked into the cylinder of the engine and ignited with a spark. The greater surface area of the mist makes it burn much faster. The rapid expansion of the gas on combustion forces the piston down the cylinder, driving the vehicle, and also forces the spent gases out through the exhaust system.

If the engine were completely efficient, all the energy in the hydrocarbon would be converted into power to drive the cylinders. At the same time, the carbon would turn into harmless carbon dioxide. No engine is very efficient, however, and the carbon does not burn up completely. As a result, carbon monoxide gas is also produced, and at the same time, some of the nitrogen naturally present in the air is converted to nitric oxide.

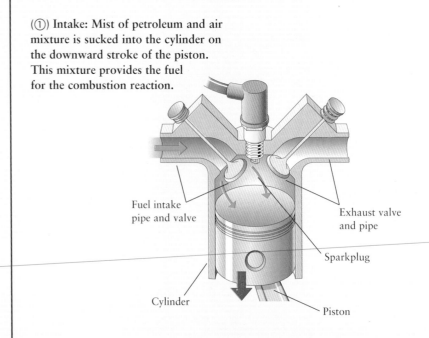

(①) Intake: Mist of petroleum and air mixture is sucked into the cylinder on the downward stroke of the piston. This mixture provides the fuel for the combustion reaction.

Fuel intake pipe and valve

Exhaust valve and pipe

Sparkplug

Cylinder

Piston

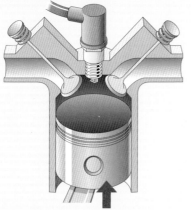

(②) **Compression:** The fuel and air mixture is compressed by the upward stroke of the piston.

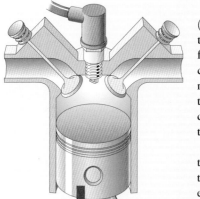

(③) **Power:** A spark from the sparkplug ignites the fuel mixture, creating a controlled explosion. The release in pressure forces the piston down the cylinder, delivering power to the engine.

The chemical energy from the combustion reaction is transferred into moving energy in the piston that, in turn, drives the engine.

(④) **Exhaust:** On the return stroke, and before new air and fuel are introduced, the exhaust valves open, and the rising piston pushes the combustion products into the exhaust system.

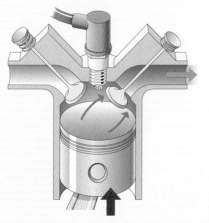

Pollution produced by combustion of fossil fuels

The fossil fuels we use in our cars and electricity-generating power stations are not just simple compounds of carbon and hydrogen. Instead, they are mixtures that contain traces of other elements such as sulfur or oxygen. Also, chemicals such as lead compounds may be added during their manufacture to alter their properties.

So, although the principal products of burning fossil fuels are carbon dioxide and water, other chemicals are produced, bringing their own problems. Gases such as carbon monoxide, sulfur oxides (known as "sox"), and nitrogen oxides (known as "nox") are produced.

The products of combustion are dependent not only on the composition of the fuel but on many other factors, including the condition of the engine, the temperature of the combustion, and the atmosphere into which they are released.

Carbon monoxide is produced by the incomplete combustion of carbon fuels (see page 40) and comes largely from motor vehicles.

Sulfur oxides come mostly from burning heavy fuels and consist of a mixture — chiefly sulfur dioxide, sulfuric acid, and various sulfate compounds. The cost of removing much of the sulfur now collected from smelters and power stations is met by using it as a raw material in other chemical industries.

Nitrogen oxides are formed when the nitrogen in air combines with oxygen in high-temperature flames during combustion and comes mostly from electricity-generating plants and motor vehicles. Although the main emission is of nitrogen monoxide (NO), it is rapidly oxidized to brown nitrogen dioxide on reaching the atmosphere, where it is an important pollutant. Nitrogen dioxide contributes to ACID RAIN and PHOTOCHEMICAL SMOG. It causes irritation to the lungs, assists in the formation of (nitrate) particles that reduce visibility, and aids the generation of ozone, which, in turn, is harmful.

A CATALYTIC CONVERTER, now attached to the exhaust of most modern vehicles, oxidizes carbon monoxide and hydrocarbons and the nitrogen oxides to produce relatively harmless emissions of nitrogen, carbon dioxide, and water.

(Above) **Photochemical smog above Los Angeles.**

Incomplete combustion

It is uncommon for combustion to be complete. Incomplete combustion is more frequent, in which only some of the reactant or reactants combust, or the products are not those that would be obtained if all the reactions went to completion, e.g., C or CO and not CO_2. The next four demonstrations illustrate incomplete combustion.

Demonstration 1: incomplete combustion of camphor vapor

Camphor contains carbon and hydrogen. When camphor boils in a boiling tube, a vapor is created at the mouth of the tube that combines with oxygen in the air and is readily ignited. It burns with a yellow, smoky flame (①) typical of DIFFUSION COMBUSTION.

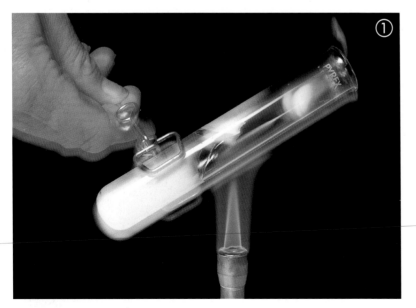

①

The yellow color is produced by tiny incandescent soot particles suspended in the air.

Notice also that the boiling camphor itself does not combust, and that it is the vapor that takes part in combustion. The fact that the combustion occurs only around the end of the tube also shows that a supply of oxygen is required for combustion. A continuous supply of oxygen would not be available within the tube. (For more on camphor, see page 12.)

Demonstration 2: pyrolysis of wood

PYROLYSIS is the name given to chemical reactions that produce liquid products from solid reactants as a result of heat. Wood is a complex carbon-based substance that decomposes, on being heated, into a variety of materials.

The apparatus consists of a can with a close-fitting lid. A small hole is made in the lid of the can, and the can is then half filled with sawdust (wood with a large surface area) (②). The can is then placed on a tripod and is strongly heated using a Bunsen flame.

The can heats quickly, and a smoky gas appears through the hole (③). Putting a Bunsen flame to this gas does not cause ignition, proving that it is non-combustible, and in fact it is mostly steam.

The steam then stops, and the gases coming from the hole now combust to provide a long jet of flame (④). The combustible gases contain hydrogen and hydrocarbons.

After a few minutes the gases cease, as all of the volatile components have been driven off. On allowing the can to cool and then opening the lid, an oily deposit is found on the inside of the can (⑤). This is a mixture of heavier molecular substances that were not volatile enough to be emitted as gases but were simply distilled out of the wood and condensed inside the tin.

The black powder making up the bulk of the remaining material in the can is charcoal (black carbon).

Remarks

The pyrolysis of wood distills out all of its hydrogen-containing components, such as steam or hydrocarbon gases. A wood fire has flames because the heat causes pyrolysis of the timber, and vapor is produced. Charcoal glows but has no flames. No pyrolysis is possible, and no fuel vapor forms.

Demonstration 3: burning a candle

A burning candle is a reaction between wax vapor (a fuel) and the oxygen of the air. A candle burning inside a gas jar goes out as soon as the oxygen is used up.

The flame above a candle is produced when the heat from the wick, and subsequently the flame, melts the solid wax, causing the molten wax to rise up the wick and form vapor, which then ignites. In igniting, the vapor combines with the oxygen of the air to form carbon dioxide gas and water vapor (steam). Some carbon, as soot particles, is also released, and this can stick to surfaces as a black deposit (⑥).

Wax is a mixture of hydrocarbons – compounds containing only carbon and hydrogen. Complete combustion converts all of the carbon to carbon dioxide and all of the hydrogen into water. This requires a plentiful supply of the oxygen found in the air around the candle. Such a condition exists and can be seen in the blue base of the flame, where an adequate supply of oxygen is supplied in the air rising by convection.

In the yellow zone of the flame there is not enough oxygen for complete combustion. Instead, incomplete combustion takes place, producing not only carbon dioxide and water but also particles of soot (mostly carbon). It is these small particles of soot being heated to a temperature at which they become incandescent that produces the yellow color.

In addition to the luminous area there is an internal cone of unburned hydrocarbon vapor, seen as the darker region inside the flame (see pages 38 and 39).

Remarks

A yellow flame present proves that there is incomplete combustion and soot produced. This is because there is a limited supply of oxygen to the vapor, and combustion can only occur where the vapor meets the air.

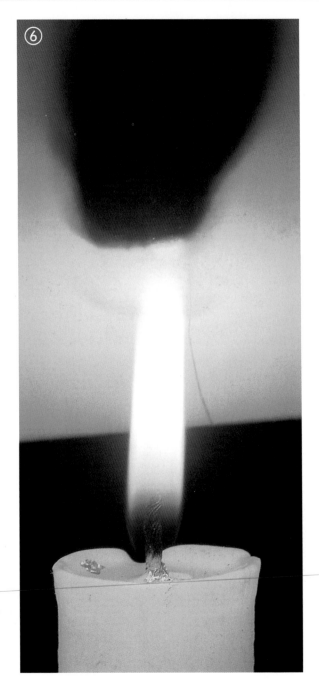

Demonstration 4: combustion in a Bunsen flame

The Bunsen burner (⑦) enables methane gas (a hydrocarbon) to be burned in a controlled way (⑧). The Bunsen burner consists of a base through which the gas enters, a vertical pipe or barrel that has a hole in the side near the base, and a collar (or sleeve) that can be rotated to cover or uncover the hole in the pipe.

When the gas tap is turned on, and gas flows up the pipe, it produces a draft that can suck air in through the hole near the base. The collar around the pipe is provided so that the amount of oxygen mixing with the methane can be controlled.

(Below) The components of a Bunsen burner allow for the controlled combustion of methane to produce a flame the temperature of which can be controlled using a valve.

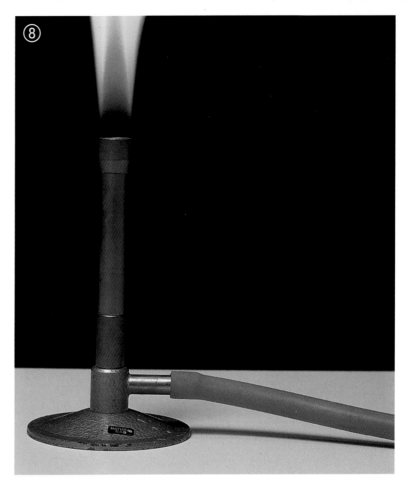

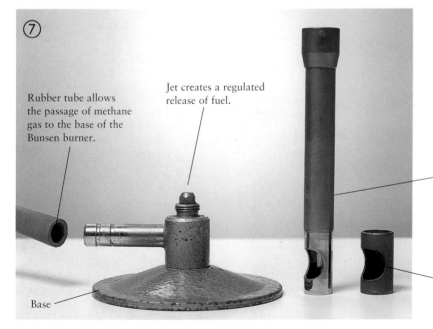

Rubber tube allows the passage of methane gas to the base of the Bunsen burner.

Jet creates a regulated release of fuel.

Base

Tube or barrel directs the flame. The barrel has a hole near the base that can allow air to be sucked in.

The collar (or sleeve) acts as a valve and can be used to regulate the supply of air, and therefore oxygen, available to mix with the methane fuel. When the valve is fully open, the maximum oxygen is supplied, and the most complete combustion occurs, producing a blue flame with the highest temperature. When the valve is closed, the oxygen supply is restricted to that surrounding the flame at the top of the barrel, and a yellow flickering flame is produced, which has a relatively low temperature.

(a) flickering yellow flame

When the air hole is closed, oxygen cannot enter the pipe, and methane and oxygen can only mix at the top of the pipe. The mixing is a diffusion combustion process, and a smoky yellow flame is formed (⑨), which is similar to a candle burning (see page 44).

In the small blue zone above the pipe there is complete combustion, and so all of the hydrogen is converted to water or steam, and all of the carbon is converted to carbon dioxide. In this region there is no carbon left over, which is why the flame is virtually colorless (slightly blue).

However, the majority of the flame is luminous yellow because here incomplete combustion is occurring; and although all of the hydrogen is converted to steam, and most of the carbon is converted to carbon dioxide, some carbon remains as soot particles, which then begin to incandesce (glow).

Remarks

The reason why you get both complete combustion and incomplete combustion is that the air hole is closed, and so only gas is coming out of the pipe. Air is drawn into the flame by convection, and the lowest part of gas near the top of the pipe uses up much of the oxygen supply, producing complete combustion. Higher up there is insufficient oxygen for complete combustion to occur, and the temperature is not high enough to produce carbon monoxide (the burning of which gives the blue color to the flame).

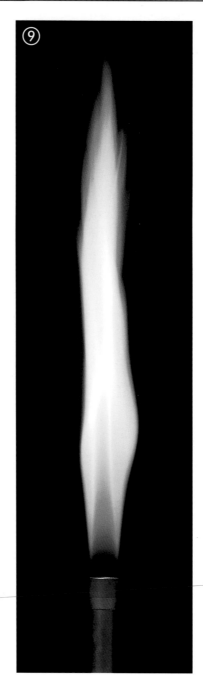

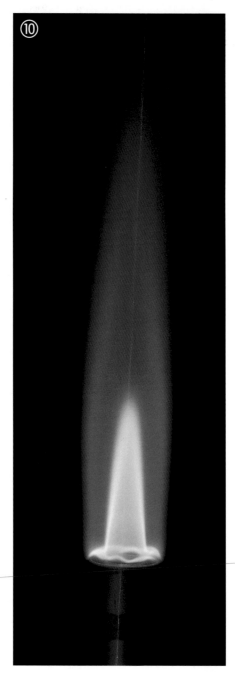

(b) blue flame

When the air hole is fully open, the oxygen and gas mix thoroughly inside the Bunsen tube or barrel so that complete combustion occurs above the pipe, and a blue, soot-free flame is produced (⑩). This is an example of MIXING COMBUSTION.

The gas-air mixture flows out of the top of the pipe faster than the flame can move back down through the mixture, which is why the flame does not move down inside the pipe. If you were to pinch the tube slightly and reduce the gas supply quickly, you might find that the flame would actually move down the burner tube to the air hole; in other words, the Bunsen burner would "strike back."

In the case of a blue flame the blue cone has unburned gas inside it. We can demonstrate this by putting one end of a small glass tube inside the blue cone (⑪) and lighting the gas that comes out of the end of the tube (⑫).

The blue zone is on the outside of the cone, where the air-gas mixture is burning most rapidly, and the hottest part of the flame is just beyond the tip of the blue cone. In the case of the blue flame there is

enough air for virtually complete combustion, so there is almost no soot and so no yellow incandescence of soot particles.

Remarks

The occasional yellow flicker occurs when particles of dust floating in the air get pulled into the Bunsen flame.

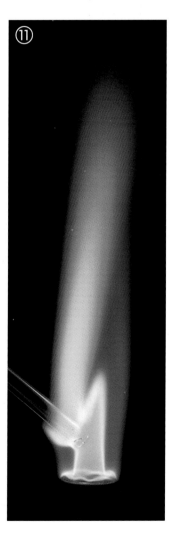

Combustion of elements that produce a flame

The next three demonstrations illustrate the complete combustion reactions in which a flame is produced. The reactions involve combustion of elements in air or in pure oxygen.

Demonstration 1: combustion of phosphorus in air

White phosphorus is an extremely reactive element in Group 5 in the Periodic Table. It is normally kept under water because exposure to air allows rapid oxidation, and spontaneous combustion follows. This particular form of phosphorus is very unstable because the molecules have formed in such a way that they already contain some energy.

The apparatus consists of a BELL JAR that will be placed in a PNEUMATIC TROUGH containing tap water (which in most areas is naturally slightly alkaline). If some UNIVERSAL INDICATOR is added to the tap water in the trough and stirred, the resulting solution becomes blue (①). The presence of the indicator will help show what is happening during the combustion reaction.

Phosphorus is supplied as sticks for use in the laboratory, and it can be cut with a spatula because it is quite soft (②). However, even chopping a small piece off a stick causes the freshly cut end to smoke, and since it can spontaneously ignite before it is replaced under water, some speed is useful at this stage.

A small piece of phosphorus is to be floated on the water inside the bell jar but kept out of contact with the water. To do this, a CRUCIBLE lid is fixed to a cork to act as a float (③).

The piece of phosphorus is then placed on the crucible lid, and the bell jar placed over the top, taking the stopper out first so that no air is trapped and the water level is the same inside the bell jar as outside in the trough. The phosphorus is now touched with a warm piece of wire through the top of the bell jar (④), and the wire withdrawn and the stopper replaced, allowing the reaction to proceed (⑤).

The phosphorus rapidly combusts, using up the oxygen and producing a white smoke of phosphoric oxide particles (⑥). At first, the heat from the flaming phosphorus makes the gas inside the bell jar expand, and so the water level will go down inside the bell jar and go up in the trough (⑦, page 50); but as the oxygen is used up, the flame is extinguished, the gas inside the bell jar cools down, and the levels will first become the same once more, then rise inside the bell jar (⑧). The white phosphorus oxide will settle either on the sides of the gas jar or actually on the water. As this happens, the color of the indicator inside the bell jar will turn to pink as the phosphoric oxide combines with the water and forms phosphoric acid. In this way it is possible to show that a portion of the air (oxygen) is used up when phosphorus combusts in it and that the product of combustion is an acidic oxide.

EQUATION: Burning white phosphorus in air
Phosphorus + oxygen ⇨ phosphorus(V) oxide
$P_4(s, white) + 5O_2(g) ⇨ P_4O_{10}(s)$

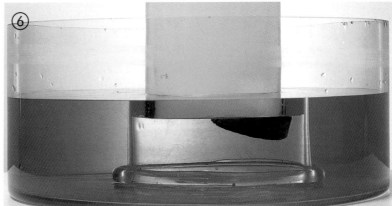

Demonstration 2: combustion of sulfur in oxygen

In this demonstration some yellow sulfur powder is placed on a combustion spoon and ignited in air. It is then introduced into a gas jar filled with oxygen (⑨), where it burns with a blue flame (⑩ & ⑪). Complete combustion occurs in which the burned sulfur reacts with the oxygen to make sulfur dioxide. Sulfur dioxide is a toxic gas, and so the demonstration is conducted in a fume chamber.

EQUATION: Burning sulfur in air
Sulfur + oxygen ⇨ sulfur dioxide
$S(s) + O_2(g) \Rightarrow SO_2(g)$

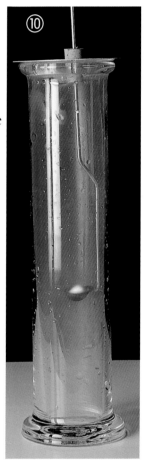

Gas jar of oxygen sealed with a glass cover slip.

A combustion spoon is a special metal spoon on a wire with a disc or collar to contain the reactants in the gas jar and to protect anyone holding the spoon from the reaction taking place. The disc also serves as a support for holding the spoon in the middle of the gas jar.

Sulfur powder

Demonstration 3: combustion of hydrogen in air

In this demonstration dry hydrogen is burned in air to show that the combustion of hydrogen in a supply of oxygen produces water.

Hydrogen is generated by reacting dilute hydrochloric acid with zinc in a conical flask (⑫). However, this reaction produces some water vapor that needs to be removed to make dry hydrogen. This is done by passing the gas over a drying agent, in this case granules of calcium chloride in a U-tube.

The resulting dry hydrogen burns with a colorless flame; but because the glass nozzle contains sodium compounds, the sodium content of the glass colors the flame yellow (⑬).

The gas from the combustion of the hydrogen is now tested for water. The flame is held in a wide-mouthed collecting vessel that is connected to a suction pump via a side-arm boiling tube (⑭). The blue cobalt chloride powder that has been placed in the bottom of the boiling tube rapidly turns pink, indicating the presence of water (⑮). The water can also be seen as condensation in the wide-mouthed collecting vessel.

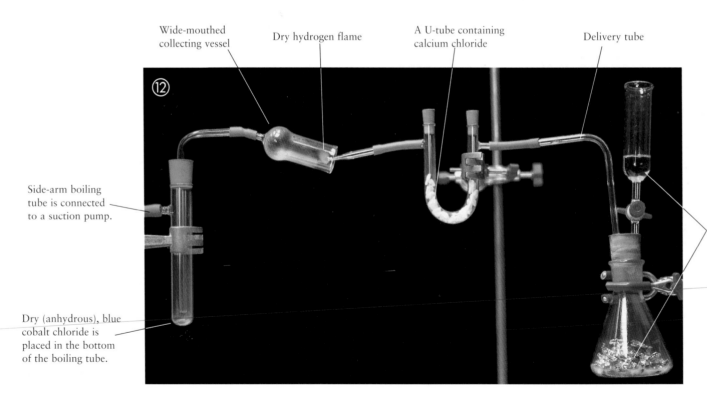

Wide-mouthed collecting vessel

Dry hydrogen flame

A U-tube containing calcium chloride

Delivery tube

Side-arm boiling tube is connected to a suction pump.

Dry (anhydrous), blue cobalt chloride is placed in the bottom of the boiling tube.

Hydrochloric acid and copper sulfate (copper catalyst) are dropped onto zinc in the conical flask, producing wet hydrogen.

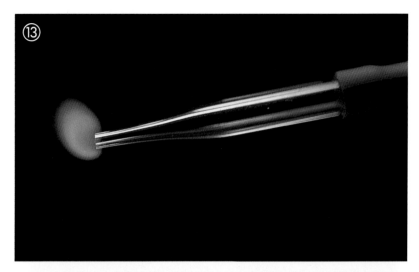

⑬

⑮

Pink, hydrated, cobalt chloride shows a positive test for the presence of water.

Remarks

An alternative, and simpler, demonstration can be made by playing the dry hydrogen flame across the base of a flask containing cold water. The water vapor, produced by the combustion of hydrogen, condenses on the cold surface of the flask (⑯).

EQUATION: Combustion of hydrogen and oxygen
Hydrogen + oxygen ⇨ water
$2H_2(g) + O_2(g) \Rightarrow 2H_2O(aq)$

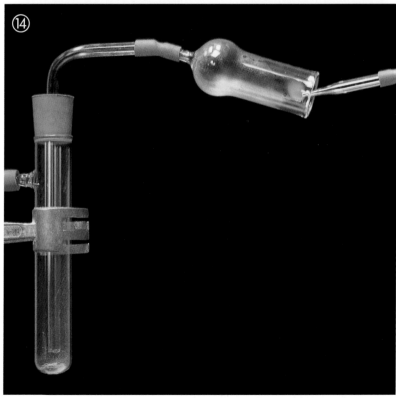

⑭

⑯

Combustion of elements that do not produce a flame

The next three examples show elements that do not give off vapors when they are heated and therefore combust in air without flames.

Demonstration 1: combustion of magnesium in air

Magnesium is in Group 2 of the Periodic Table, and so it is a reactive metal that can easily be ignited to combust in air. Magnesium is a shiny metal, but when stored in the laboratory, it reacts with the oxygen in air sufficiently to produce a dull magnesium oxide coating (①). The end of this coil of magnesium ribbon has been cleaned with emery paper to show the nature of the untarnished metal.

A piece of the magnesium ribbon was then held in metal tongs and ignited using a glowing splint. The magnesium combusts with an intense white light (②). The end of the ribbon can be seen to melt just before it ignites (melting point 650°C, boiling point 1100°C). During combustion the shiny metallic magnesium is oxidized to white magnesium oxide.

Magnesium powder was the fuel for the early flash-lights used by photographers. It was ignited by a heated filament.

Calcium (melting point 838°C, boiling point 1440°C) is much more difficult to ignite in air.

Magnesium ribbon cleaned with emery paper

Magnesium oxide

Magnesium ribbon with dull oxide coating

①

②

Demonstration 2: combustion of carbon in oxygen and air

When a piece of carbon, in the form of charcoal, is heated in air in a Bunsen burner flame, it glows (③), indicating that combustion is taking place. However, when the hot charcoal is placed in a gas jar containing oxygen, the charcoal combusts far more strongly, and a ball of white-hot carbon is produced (④). Notice, however, that despite the spectacular nature of this combustion, no flames are produced because there is only one gas involved. In the complete combustion of charcoal, carbon dioxide is the only product of the reaction. (For the result of incomplete combustion see page 56.)

It is possible to test for the presence of the carbon dioxide using limewater, which can be poured into the bottom of the gas jar. Although the limewater remains colorless when shaken with the oxygen, it turns cloudy in the presence of carbon dioxide (⑤).

EQUATION: combustion of carbon in oxygen
Carbon + oxygen ⇨ carbon dioxide
$C(s) + O_2(g) \Rightarrow CO_2(g)$

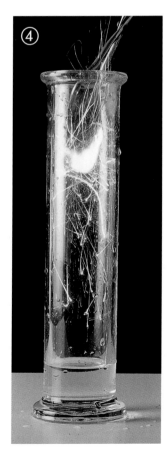

Combustion of coke

Coke is a SMOKELESS FUEL used for heating. It is used in braziers, barbecues, and home fires. Coal, too, is used for heating but behaves differently from coke when it combusts in air due to its chemical composition.

Coal is a mixture of compounds containing C, H, N, and S; and when it combusts, it gives off vapors that produce a flame. In contrast, coke is almost pure carbon, and when burned in a plentiful supply of oxygen, glows brightly but does not produce a flame (see page 55). The carbon dioxide produced is not flammable.

In a brazier, where the pieces of coke are packed quite close to one another, the supply of oxygen is restricted. In these circumstances incomplete combustion occurs, and carbon monoxide is formed in some regions within the fire as well as carbon dioxide. The toxic carbon monoxide gas burns with a characteristic blue flame and can usually be seen within and just above the brazier. As it rises further, the carbon monoxide then reacts with the oxygen in the air above the brazier and is converted to nontoxic carbon dioxide gas.

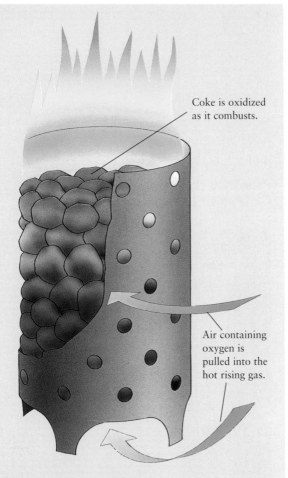

Coke is oxidized as it combusts.

Air containing oxygen is pulled into the hot rising gas.

(Below) When a lighted splint (left) is plunged into a gas jar containing carbon dioxide gas, the splint is extinguished (right), demonstrating that carbon dioxide does not support combustion.

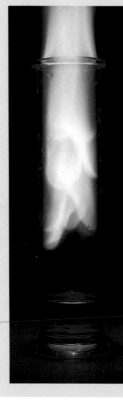

(Left) Carbon monoxide combusts readily and burns with a characteristic blue flame.

EQUATION: Coke is oxidized as it combusts
Carbon + oxygen ⇨ carbon dioxide
$C(s) + O_2(g) \Rightarrow CO_2(g)$

EQUATION: Carbon dioxide is reduced in limited supply of oxygen
Carbon dioxide + carbon ⇨ carbon monoxide
$CO_2(g) + C(s) \Rightarrow 2CO(g)$

EQUATION: Carbon monoxide oxidized in air above brazier
Carbon monoxide + oxygen ⇨ carbon dioxide
$2CO(g) + O_2(g) \Rightarrow 2CO_2(g)$

Demonstration 3: combustion of iron in oxygen and air

In this demonstration iron is used in the form of steel wool. The strands in the steel wool present a large surface area to the surrounding gas. The steel wool is held in the metal tongs (⑥) and heated strongly by a Bunsen flame (⑦). Because there is insufficient oxygen in air, the steel wool will simply glow red-hot.

When the heated steel wool is placed in a gas jar of oxygen, the combustion reaction is quite violent. With the high temperature involved, the iron glows white-hot, and sparks are produced (⑧). However, there are no vapors given off by the steel wool, and so no flame is produced. Complete combustion occurs between the oxygen available and the iron, and so iron(III) oxide is produced.

Some tap water was poured into the bottom of the gas jar so that the molten iron would not crack the gas jar.

EQUATION: Burning steel wool
Iron + oxygen ⇨ iron(III) oxide
$4Fe(s) + 3O_2(g) ⇨ 2Fe_2O_3(s)$

Combustion with the halogens

The halogens are all oxidizing agents. Many substances will combust in the presence of halogens and even produce flames (see page 37). The next four demonstrations illustrate this with the halogens chlorine and iodine, using metals as fuels.

All the halogens are toxic, and so these demonstrations are conducted in a fume chamber.

Demonstration 1: combustion of sodium in chlorine

A gas jar of distinctively green chlorine gas is first prepared by reacting concentrated hydrochloric acid and potassium permanganate. Because chlorine is more dense than air and it is also soluble in water, the gas is collected by upward displacement of air (①).

Sodium is a relatively reactive metal and will combust in air and so is normally stored under oil (②). A small pellet of sodium is placed in a crucible on a combustion spoon (③) and heated in air with a Bunsen flame until it begins to burn. The burning sodium is now lowered into the gas jar containing the chlorine. Because chlorine is a very reactive oxidizing gas, the sodium continues to combust (④). As the sodium burns, flames are produced, and a white smoke is formed (⑤). This is a cloud of tiny solid particles of sodium chloride, a halide salt. The sodium chloride gradually settles out on the walls and bottom of the gas jar and in the bowl of the combustion spoon (⑥).

EQUATION: Sodium combusts in chlorine
Sodium + chlorine ⇨ sodium chloride
$2Na(s) + Cl_2(g) \rightarrow 2NaCl(s)$

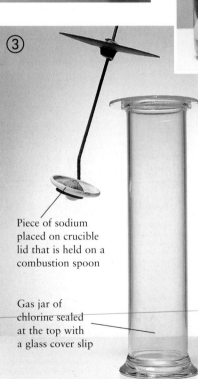

Sodium pellet

Piece of sodium placed on crucible lid that is held on a combustion spoon

Gas jar of chlorine sealed at the top with a glass cover slip

④

⑤

⑥

Sodium chloride

Demonstration 2: combustion of iron with chlorine

Iron is a less reactive metal than the sodium used in the previous demonstration and will react only slowly in air unless heated (see page 57).

In this demonstration chlorine is produced by dripping concentrated hydrochloric acid onto potassium permanganate that has been placed in a conical flask (①). This flask is connected to a combustion tube (a tube made of a heat-resistant glass) in which the iron (in the form of steel wool) has been placed. The combustion tube in turn is passed through a sealed stopper to open out into a side-arm flask that is attached to a water pump. The pump is used to draw the chlorine through the apparatus and also remove any unreacted gas.

While the chlorine is passed over the steel wool, the combustion tube is strongly heated (②). Eventually the iron ignites, producing a yellow and red glow and a red-brown smoke (③).

The Bunsen flame can be taken away at this stage because the reaction is exothermic and produces sufficient internal heat to continue the reaction unaided, the burning section slowly making its way along the tube as the iron is consumed (④).

The reddish-brown smoke, containing tiny iron chloride particles, flows out to the collecting flask, gradually condensing in the flask (⑤).

EQUATION: Combustion of iron in chlorine
Iron + chlorine ⇨ iron(III) chloride
$$2Fe(s) + 3Cl_2(g) ⇨ 2FeCl_3(s)$$

The dropper funnel allows for a controlled release of hydrochloric acid onto the potassium permanganate in the conical flask to regulate the production of chlorine.

A suction pump draws off waste fumes from a side-arm flask.

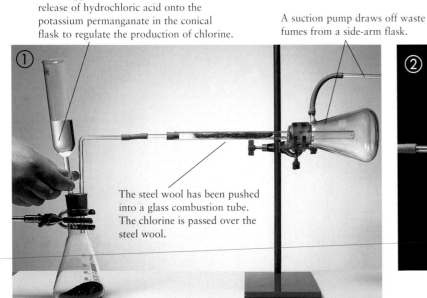

The steel wool has been pushed into a glass combustion tube. The chlorine is passed over the steel wool.

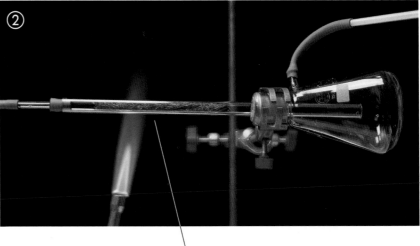

The steel wool is heated with a Bunsen burner until it ignites and is then left to combust in the chloride.

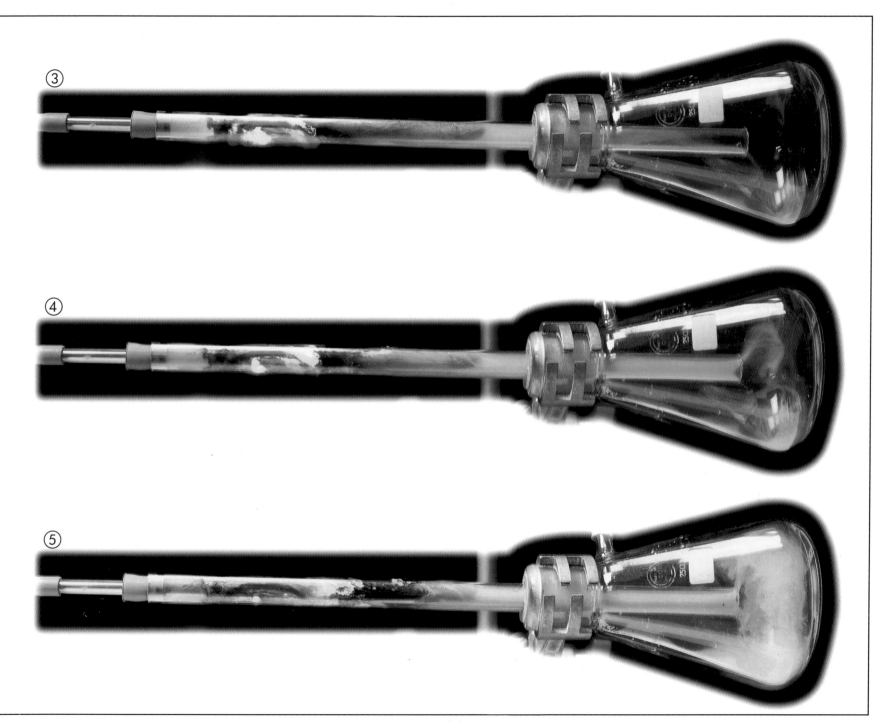

Demonstration 3: combustion of Dutch metal in chlorine

A gas jar of chlorine is first prepared as described in the demonstration on page 58.

A small amount of copper in the form of finely divided Dutch metal sheet is gripped between a pair of metal tongs (⑥) and lowered into the chlorine. The Dutch metal combusts instantly (⑦) to produce fine particles of copper(II) chloride, which are seen as a dense yellow smoke (⑧). Copper is less reactive than sodium and iron, and no flames — only a brief red flash — of light is produced during combustion.

EQUATION: Copper combusts in chlorine

Chlorine + copper ⇨ copper(II) chloride

$Cl_2(g) + Cu(s) ⇨ CuCl_2(s)$

⑧

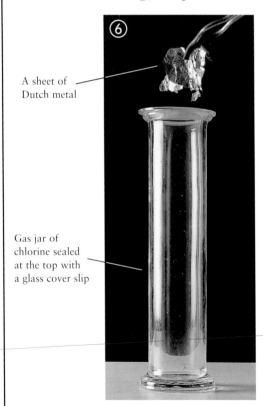
⑥

A sheet of Dutch metal

Gas jar of chlorine sealed at the top with a glass cover slip

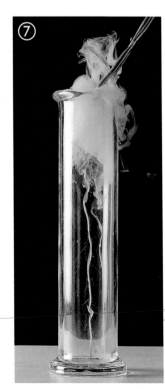
⑦

Demonstration 4: combustion with iodine

In this demonstration the oxidizing agent is the halogen iodine, as opposed to chlorine.

Some aluminum powder is added to a small pile of iodine crystals on a gauze disc, and the powder and crystals mixed gently together (⑨). In this dry state nothing happens. However, when distilled water is dropped onto the mixture (⑩) from a pipette, a combustion reaction occurs that produces dense purple iodine fumes (⑪ & ⑫). The aluminum is oxidized to an off-white deposit of aluminum(III) iodide, which is left on the gauze.

Remarks

In this reaction the water acts as a catalyst for combustion. The reaction can also be started by friction between the reactants. To avoid this problem, mixing is done gently and with care.

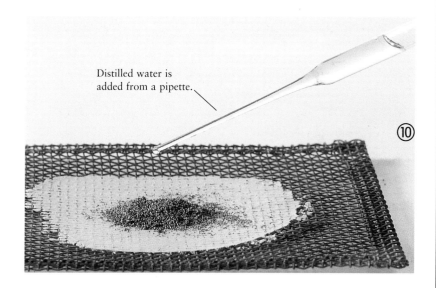

Distilled water is added from a pipette.

⑩

Iodine vapor is released due to the heat of the reaction.

⑪

EQUATION: Reaction of aluminum and iodine

Aluminum + iodine ⇨ aluminum(III) iodide

$2Al(s) + 3I_2(g) \rightarrow 2AlI_3(s)$

Heat given out

⑨ Iodine crystals   Aluminum powder

⑫

63

Spontaneous combustion

Spontaneous combustion occurs when a material oxidizes *very quickly* to produce an exothermic reaction after a period of apparent inactivity, known as an INDUCTION PERIOD.

Demonstration: mixing ethylene glycol and potassium permanganate

In this demonstration potassium permanganate is used as the oxidizing agent, and ethylene glycol (1,2-ethandiol) as the fuel. Neither of these reactants can readily be made to ignite on their own, but when mixed, combustion occurs. The demonstration should be conducted in a fume chamber.

Some potassium permanganate crystals are placed in a small pile on a heat-proof surface, and a few drops of ethylene glycol are added (①). When first mixed, nothing appears to happen because the chemicals need time to react. However, the temperature of the mixture rises until it is high enough for the ethylene glycol to ignite (②). The time taken for the ignition temperature to be reached is called the induction period, and in this demonstration it takes a minute or two. Once ignited, flames are thrown out from the reactants so that they appear to burst into flame spontaneously (③).

Purple potassium permanganate crystals

Ethylene glycol

①

②

③

EQUATION: Ethylene glycol and potassium permanganate
Ethylene glycol + oxidizing agent ⇨ *carbon dioxide + water*
$C_2H_6O_2(l)$ + 5O (from oxidizing agent) ⇨ $2CO_2(g)$ + $3H_2O(l)$

MASTER GLOSSARY

absolute zero: the lowest possible temperature ($-273.15°C$).

absorption: the process by which a substance is soaked up. *See:* adsorption.

acid: a substance that can give a proton to another substance. Acids are compounds containing hydrogen that can attack and dissolve many substances. Acids are described as weak or strong, dilute or concentrated, mineral or organic. *Example:* hydrochloric acid (HCl). An acid in water can react with a base to form a salt and water.

acidic solution: a solution with a pH lower than 7. *See:* pH.

acidity: a general term for the strength of an acid in a solution.

acid radical: the negative ion left behind when an acid loses a hydrogen ion. *Example:* Cl^- in hydrochloric acid (HCl).

acid salt: An ACID SALT contains at least one hydrogen ion and can behave as an acid in chemical reactions. Acid salts are produced under conditions that do not allow complete neutralization of the acid. For example, sulfuric acid may react with a sodium compound to produce a normal sodium salt, sodium sulfate (Na_2SO_4), or it may retain some of the hydrogen, in which case it becomes the salt sodium hydrogen sulfate ($NaHSO_4$).

actinide series or actinide metals: a series of 15 similar radioactive elements between actinium and lawrencium. They are transition metals.

activated charcoal: a form of carbon made of tiny crystals of graphite that is made by heating organic matter in the absence of air. It is then further processed to increase its pore space and therefore its surface area. Its surface area is about 2000 m^2/g. Activated charcoal readily adsorbs many gases, and it is therefore widely used as a filter, for example, in gas masks.

activation energy: the energy required to make a reaction occur. The greater the activation energy of a reaction, the more its reaction rate depends on temperature. The activation energy of a reaction is useful because, if the rate of reaction is known at one temperature (for example, 100 °C) then the activation energy can be used to calculate the rate of reaction at another temperature (for example, at 400 °C) without actually doing the experiment.

adsorption: the process by which a surface adsorbs a substance. The substances involved are not chemically combined and can be separated. *See:* absorption.

alchemy: the traditional "art" of working with chemicals common in the Middle Ages. One of the main challenges for alchemists was to make gold from lead. Alchemy faded away as scientific chemistry was developed in the 17th century.

alcohol: an organic compound that contains a hydroxyl (OH) group. *Example:* ethanol (CH_3CH_2OH), also known as ethyl alcohol or grain alcohol.

alkali/alkaline: a base in (aqueous) solution. Alkalis react with or neutralize hydrogen ions in acids and have a pH greater than 7.0 because they contain relatively few hydrogen ions. *Example:* aqueous sodium hydroxide (NaOH). *See:* pH.

alkaline cell (or battery): a dry cell in which the electrolyte contains sodium or potassium hydroxide.

alkaline earth metal: a member of Group 2 of the Periodic Table. *Example:* calcium.

alkali metals: a member of Group 1 of the Periodic Table. *Example:* sodium.

alkane: a hydrocarbon with no carbon-to-carbon multiple bonds. *Example:* ethane, C_2H_6.

alkene: a hydrocarbon with at least one carbon-to-carbon double bond. *Example:* ethylene, C_2H_4.

alkyne: a hydrocarbon with at least one carbon-to-carbon triple bond. *Example:* acetylene, C_2H_2.

allotropes: alternative forms of an element that differ in the way the atoms are linked. *Example:* white and red phosphorus.

alloy: a mixture of a metal and various other elements. *Example:* brass is an alloy of copper and zinc.

amalgam: a liquid alloy of mercury with another metal.

amorphous: a solid in which the atoms are not arranged regularly (i.e., "glassy"). Compare crystalline.

amphoteric: a metal that will react with both acids and alkalis. *Example:* aluminum metal.

anhydrous: lacking water; water has been removed, for example by heating. (Opposite of anhydrous is hydrous or hydrated.) *Example:* copper(II) sulfate can be anhydrous ($CuSO_4$) or hydrated ($CuSO_4 \cdot 5H_2O$).

anion: a negatively charged atom or group of atoms. *Examples:* chloride ion (Cl^-), hydroxide ion (OH^-).

anode: the electrode at which oxidation occurs; the negative terminal of a battery or the positive electrode of an electrolysis cell.

anodizing: a process that uses the effect of electrolysis to make a surface corrosion-resistant. *Example:* anodized aluminum.

antacid: a common name for any compound that reacts with stomach acid to neutralize it. *Example:* sodium hydrogen carbonate, also known as sodium bicarbonate.

antioxidant: a substance that reacts rapidly with radicals, thereby preventing oxidation of some other substance.

antibumping granules: small glass or ceramic beads designed to promote boiling without the development of large gas bubbles.

approximate relative atomic mass: *See:* relative atomic mass.

aqueous: a solution in which the solvent is water. Usually used as "aqueous solution." *Example:* aqueous solution of sodium hydroxide (NaOH(aq)).

aromatic hydrocarbons: compounds of carbon that have the benzene ring as part of their structure. *Examples:* benzene (C_6H_6), naphthalene ($C_{10}H_8$). They are known as aromatic because of their strong pungent smell.

atmospheric pressure: the pressure exerted by the gases in the air. Units of measurement are kilopascals (kPa), atmospheres (atm), millimeters of mercury (mm Hg), and Torr. Standard atmospheric pressure is 100 kPa, 1 atm, 760 mm Hg or 760 Torr.

atom: the smallest particle of an element; a nucleus and its surrounding electrons.

atomic mass: the mass of an atom measured in atomic mass units (u). An atomic mass unit equals one twelfth of the atom of carbon-12. "Atomic mass" is now more generally used than "atomic weight." *Example:* the atomic mass of chlorine is about 35 u. *See:* atomic weight, relative atomic mass.

atomic number: also known as proton number. The number of electrons or the number of protons in an atom. *Example:* the atomic number of gold is 79.

atomic structure: the nucleus and the arrangement of electrons around it.

atomic weight: a common term used to mean the average molar mass of an element (g/mol). This is the mass per mole of atoms. *Example:* the atomic weight of chlorine is about 35 g/mol. *See:* atomic mass, mole.

base: a substance that can accept a proton from another substance. *Example:* aqueous ammonia ($NH_3(aq)$). A base can react with an acid in water to form a salt and water.

basic salt: a salt that contains at least one hydroxide ion. The hydroxide ion can then behave as a base in chemical reactions. *Example:* the reaction of hydrochloric acid (HCl) with the base aluminum hydroxide ($Al(OH)_3$) can form two basic salts, $Al(OH)_2Cl$ and $Al(OH)Cl_2$.

battery: a number of electrochemical cells placed in series.

bauxite: a hydrated impure oxide of aluminum ($Al_2O_3 \cdot xH_2O$, with the amount of water x being variable). It is the main ore used to obtain aluminum metal. The reddish brown color of bauxite is mainly caused by the iron oxide impurities it contains.

beehive shelf: an inverted earthenware bowl with a hole in the upper surface and a slot in the rim. Traditionally the earthenware was brown and looked similar to a beehive, hence its name. A delivery tube passes through the slot, and a gas jar is placed over the hole. This provides a convenient way to collect gas over water in a pneumatic trough.

bell jar: a tall glass jar with an open bottom and a wide, stoppered neck that is used in conjunction with a beehive shelf and a pneumatic trough in some experiments involving gases. The name derives from historic versions of the apparatus, which resembled a bell in shape.

blast furnace: a tall furnace charged with a mixture of iron ore, coke, and limestone and used for the refining of iron metal. The name comes from the strong blast of air introduced during smelting.

bleach: a substance that removes color from stains on materials either by oxidizing or reducing the staining compound. *Example:* sulfur dioxide (SO_2).

block: one of the main divisions of the Periodic Table. Blocks are named for the outermost occupied electron shell of an element. *Example:* the Transition Metals all belong to the d-block.

boiling point: the temperature at which a liquid boils, changing from a liquid to a gas. Boiling points change with atmospheric pressure. *Example:* The boiling point of pure water at standard atmospheric pressure is 100 °C.

boiling tube: A thin glass tube closed at one end and used for chemical tests. The composition and thickness of the glass is such that it cannot sustain very high temperatures and is intended for heating liquids to boiling point. *See:* side-arm boiling tube, test tube.

bond: chemical bonding is either a transfer or sharing of electrons by two or more atoms. There are a number of types of chemical bond, some very strong (such as covalent and ionic bonds), others weak (such as hydrogen bonds). Chemical bonds form because the linked molecule is more stable than the unlinked atoms from which it formed. *Example:* the hydrogen molecule (H_2) is more stable than single atoms of hydrogen, which is why hydrogen gas is always found as molecules of two hydrogen atoms.

Boyle's Law: At constant temperature, and for a given mass of gas, the volume of the gas (V) is inversely proportional to pressure that builds up (P): $P \propto 1/V$.

brine: a solution of salt (sodium chloride, NaCl) in water.

Büchner flask: a thick-walled side-arm flask designed to withstand the changes in pressure that occur when the flask is connected to a suction pump.

Büchner funnel: a special design of plastic or ceramic funnel that has a flat stage on which a filter paper can be placed. It is intended for use under suction with a Büchner funnel.

buffer (solution): a mixture of substances in solution that resists a change in the acidity or alkalinity of the solution when small amounts of an acid or alkali are added.

burette: a long, graduated glass tube with a tap at one end. A burette is used vertically, with the tap lowermost, as a reservoir for a chemical during titration.

burn: a combustion reaction in which a flame is produced. A flame occurs where *gases* combust and release heat and light. At least two gases are therefore required if there is to be a flame. *Example:* methane gas (CH_4) burns in oxygen gas (O_2) to produce carbon dioxide (CO_2) and water (H_2O) and give out heat and light.

calorimeter: an insulated container designed to prevent heat gain or loss with the environment and thus allow changes of temperature within reacting chemicals to be measured accurately. It is named after the old unit of heat, the calorie.

capillary: a very small diameter (glass) tube. Capillary tubing has a small enough diameter to allow surface tension effects to retain water within the tube.

capillary action: the tendency for a liquid to be sucked into small spaces, such as between objects and through narrow-pore tubes. The force to do this comes from surface tension.

carbohydrate: a compound containing only carbon, hydrogen and oxygen. Carbohydrates have the formula $C_n(H_2O)_n$, where n is variable. *Example:* glucose ($C_6H_{12}O_6$).

carbonate: a salt of carbonic acid. Carbonate ions have the chemical formula CO_3^{2-}. *Examples:* calcium nitrate $CaCO_3$ and sodium carbonate Na_2CO_3.

catalyst: a substance that speeds up a chemical reaction but itself remains unaltered at the end of the reaction. *Example:* copper in the reaction of hydrochloric acid with zinc.

catalytic converter: a device incorporated into some exhaust systems. The catalytic converter contains a framework or granules with a very large surface area and coated with catalysts that convert the pollutant gases passing over them into harmless products.

cathode: the electrode at which reduction occurs; the positive terminal of a battery or the negative electrode of an electrolysis cell.

cathodic protection: the technique of protecting a metal object by connecting it to a more readily oxidizable metal. The metal object being protected is made into the cathode of a cell. *Example:* iron can be protected by coupling it with magnesium. Iron forms the cathode and magnesium the anode.

cation: a positively charged ion. *Examples:* calcium ion (Ca^{2+}), ammonium ion (NH_4^+).

caustic: a substance that can cause burns if it touches the skin. *Example:* Sodium hydroxide, caustic soda (NaOH).

Celsius scale (°C): a temperature scale on which the freezing point of water is at 0 degrees, and the normal boiling point at standard atmospheric pressure is 100 degrees.

cell: a vessel containing two electrodes and an electrolyte that can act as an electrical conductor.

centrifuge: an instrument for spinning small samples very rapidly. The fast spin makes the components of a mixture that have a different density separate, as in filtration.

ceramic: a material based on clay minerals that has been heated so that it has chemically hardened.

chalcogens: the members of Group 6 of the Periodic Table: oxygen, sulfur, selenium and tellurium. The word comes from the Greek meaning "brass giver," because all these elements are found in copper ores, and copper is the most important metal in making brass.

change of state: a change between two of the three states of matter, solid, liquid, and gas. *Example:* when water evaporates it changes from a liquid to a gaseous state.

Charles's Law: The volume (V) of a given mass of gas at constant pressure is directly proportional to its absolute temperature (T): $V \propto T$.

chromatography: A separation technique uses the ability of surfaces to adsorb substances with different strengths. The substances with the least adherence to the surface move faster and leave behind those that adhere more strongly.

coagulation: a term describing the tendency of small particles to stick together in clumps.

coherent: meaning that a substance holds together or sticks together well, and without holes or other defects. *Example:* Aluminum appears unreactive because, as soon as new metal is exposed to air, it forms a very complete oxide coating, which then stops further reaction occurring.

coinage metals: the elements copper, silver, and gold, used to make coins.

coke: a solid substance left after the gases have been extracted from coal.

colloid: a mixture of ultramicroscopic particles dispersed uniformly through a second substance to form a suspension that may be almost like a solution or may set to a jelly (gel). The word comes from the Greek for glue.

colorimeter: an instrument for measuring the light-absorbing power of a substance. The absorption gives an accurate indication of the concentration of some colored solutions.

combustion: a reaction in which an element or compound is oxidized to release energy. Some combustion reactions are slow, such as the combustion of the sugar we eat to provide energy. If the combustion results in a flame, it is called burning. A flame occurs where *gases* combust and release heat and light. At least two gases are therefore required if there is to be a flame. *Example:* the combustion or burning of methane gas (CH_4) in oxygen gas (O_2) produces carbon dioxide (CO_2)

and water (H_2O) and gives out heat and light. Some combustion reactions produce light and heat but do not produce flames. *Example:* the combustion of carbon in oxygen produces an intense red-white light but no flame.

combustion spoon: also known as a deflagrating spoon, it consists of a long metal handle with a small cup at the end. Its purpose is to allow the safe introduction of a (usually heated) substance into a filled gas jar, when the reaction is likely to be vigorous. *Example:* the introduction of a heated sodium pellet into a gas jar containing chlorine.

compound: a chemical consisting of two or more elements chemically bonded together. *Example:* Calcium atoms can combine with carbon atoms and oxygen atoms to make calcium carbonate ($CaCO_3$), a compound of all three atoms.

condensation: the formation of a liquid from a gas. This is a change of state, also called a phase change.

condensation nuclei: microscopic particles of dust, salt, and other materials suspended in the air that attract water molecules. The usual result is the formation of water droplets.

condensation polymer: a polymer formed by a chain of reactions in which a water molecule is eliminated as every link of the polymer is formed. *Examples:* polyesters, proteins, nylon.

conduction: (i) the exchange of heat (heat conduction) by contact with another object, or (ii) allowing the flow of electrons (electrical conduction).

conductivity: the ability of a substance to conduct. The conductivity of a solution depends on there being suitable free ions in the solution. A conducting solution is called an electrolyte. *Example:* dilute sulfuric acid.

convection: the exchange of heat energy with the surroundings produced by the flow of a fluid due to being heated or cooled.

corrosion: the oxidation of a metal. Corrosion is often regarded as unwanted and is more generally used to refer to the *slow* decay of a metal resulting from contact with gases and liquids in the environment. *Example:* Rust is the corrosion of iron.

corrosive: causing corrosion. *Example:* Sodium hydroxide (NaOH).

covalent bond: this is the most common form of strong chemical bonding and occurs when two atoms *share* electrons. *Example:* oxygen (O_2)

cracking: breaking down complex molecules into simpler compounds, as in oil refining.

crucible: a small bowl with a lip, made of heat-resistant white glazed ceramic. It is used for heating substances using a Bunsen flame.

crude oil: a chemical mixture of petroleum liquids. Crude oil forms the raw material for an oil refinery.

crystal: a substance that has grown freely so that it can develop external faces. Compare with crystalline, where the atoms are not free to form individual crystals, and amorphous, where the atoms are arranged irregularly.

crystalline: a solid in which the atoms, ions, or molecules are organized into an orderly pattern without distinct crystal faces. *Examples:* copper(II) sulfate, sodium chloride. Compare amorphous.

crystallization: the process in which a solute comes out of solution slowly and forms crystals. *See:* water of crystallization.

crystal systems: seven patterns or systems into which all crystals can be grouped: cubic, hexagonal, rhombohedral, tetragonal, orthorhombic, monoclinic, and triclinic.

cubic crystal system: groupings of crystals that look like cubes.

current: an electric current is produced by a flow of electrons through a conducting solid or ions through a conducting liquid. The rate of supply of this charge is measured in amperes (A).

decay (radioactive decay): the way that a radioactive element changes into another element due to loss of mass through radiation. *Example:* uranium 238 decays with the loss of an alpha particle to form thorium 234.

decomposition: the break down of a substance (for example, by heat or with the aid of a catalyst) into simpler components. In such a chemical reaction only one substance is involved. *Example:* hydrogen peroxide ($H_2O_2(aq)$) into oxygen ($O_2(g)$) and water ($H_2O(l)$).

decrepitation: when, as part of the decomposition of a substance, cracking sounds are also produced. *Example:* heating of lead nitrate ($Pb(NO_3)_2$).

dehydration: the removal of water from a substance by heating it, placing it in a dry atmosphere, or using a drying (dehydrating) reagent such as concentrated sulfuric acid.

density: the mass per unit volume (e.g., g/cc).

desalinization: the removal of all the salts from sea water, by reverse osmosis or heating the water and collecting the distillate. It is a very energy-intensive process.

desiccant: a substance that absorbs water vapor from the air. *Example:* silica gel.

desiccator: a lidded glass bowl containing a shelf. The apparatus is designed to store materials in dry air. A desiccant is placed below the shelf, and the substance to be dried is placed on the shelf. The lid makes a gas-tight joint with the bowl.

destructive distillation: the heating of a material so that it decomposes entirely to release all of its volatile components. Destructive distillation is also known as pyrolysis.

detergent: a chemical based on petroleum that removes dirt.

Devarda's alloy: zinc with a trace of copper that acts as a catalyst for reactions with the zinc.

diaphragm: a semipermeable membrane – a kind of ultrafine mesh filter – that allows only small ions to pass through. It is used in the electrolysis of brine.

diffusion: the slow mixing of one substance with another until the two substances are evenly mixed. Mixing occurs because of differences in concentration within the mixture. Diffusion works rapidly with gases, very slowly with liquids.

diffusion combustion: the form of combustion that occurs when two gases just begin to mix during ignition. As a result, the flame is hollow and yellow in color. *Example:* a candle flame.

dilute acid: an acid whose concentration has been reduced in a large proportion of water.

disinfectant: a chemical that kills bacteria and other microorganisms.

displacement reaction: a reaction that occurs because metals differ in their reactivity. If a more reactive metal is placed in a solution of a less reactive metal compound, a reaction occurs in which the more reactive metal displaces the metal ions in the solution. *Example:* when zinc metal is introduced into a solution of copper(II) sulfate (which thus contains copper ions), zinc goes into solution as zinc ions, while copper is displaced from the solution and forced to precipitate as metallic copper.

dissociate: to break bonds apart. In the case of acids it means to break up forming hydrogen ions. This is an example of ionization. Strong acids dissociate completely. Weak acids are not completely ionized, and a solution of a weak acid has a relatively low concentration of hydrogen ions.

dissolve: to break down a substance in a solution without causing a reaction.

distillation: the process of separating mixtures by condensing the vapors through cooling.

distilled water: distilled water is nearly pure water and is produced by distillation of tap water. Distilled water is used in the laboratory in preference to tap water because the distillation process removes many of the impurities in tap water that may influence the chemical reactions for which the water is used.

Dreschel bottle: a tall bottle with a special stopper designed to allow a gas to pass through a liquid. The stopper contains both inlet and outlet tubes. One tube extends below the surface of the liquid so that the gas has to pass through the liquid before it can escape to the outlet tube.

dropper funnel: a special funnel with a tap to allow the controlled release of a liquid. Also known as a dropping funnel or tap funnel.

drying agent: *See:* dehydrating agent.

dye: a colored substance that will stick to another substance so that both appear colored.

effervesce: to give off bubbles of gas.

effloresce: to lose water and turn to a fine powder on exposure to the air. *Example:* Sodium carbonate on the rim of a reagent bottle stopper.

electrical conductivity: *See:* conductivity

electrical potential: the energy produced by an electrochemical cell and measured by the voltage or electromotive force (emf). *See:* potential difference, electromotive force.

electrochemical cell: a cell consisting of two electrodes and an electrolyte. It can be set up to generate an electric current (usually known as a galvanic cell, an example of which is a battery), or an electric current can be passed through it to produce a chemical reaction (in which case it is called an electrolytic cell and can be used to refine metals or for electroplating).

electrochemical series: the arrangement of substances that are either oxidizing or reducing agents in order of strength as a reagent, for example, with the strong oxidizing agents at the top of the list and the strong reducing agents at the bottom.

electrode: a conductor that forms one terminal of a cell.

electrolysis: an electrical-chemical process that uses an electric current to cause the breakup of a compound and the movement of metal ions in a solution. The process happens in many natural situations (as for example in rusting) and is also commonly used in industry for purifying (refining) metals or for plating metal objects with a fine, even metal coating.

electrolyte: an ionic solution that conducts electricity.

electrolytic cell: *See:* electrochemical cell

electromotive force (emf): the force set up in an electric circuit by a potential difference.

electron: a tiny, negatively charged particle that is part of an atom. The flow of electrons through a solid

material such as a wire produces an electric current.

electron configuration: the pattern in which electrons are arranged in shells around the nucleus of an atom. *Example:* chlorine has the configuration 2, 8, 7.

electroplating: depositing a thin layer of a metal onto the surface of another substance using electrolysis.

element: a substance that cannot be decomposed into simpler substance by chemical means. *Examples:* calcium, iron, gold.

emulsion: tiny droplets of one substance dispersed in another. One common oil in water emulsion is called milk. Because the tiny droplets tend to come together, another stabilizing substance is often needed. Soaps and detergents are such agents, wrapping the particles of grease and oil in a stable coat. Photographic film is an example of a solid emulsion.

endothermic reaction: a reaction that takes in heat. *Example:* when ammonium chloride is dissolved in water.

end point: the stage in a titration when the reaction between the titrant (added from a burette) and the titrate (in the flask) is complete. The end point is normally recognized by use of an indicator that has been added to the titrate. In an acid-base reaction this is also called the neutralization point.

enzyme: biological catalysts in the form of proteins in the body that speed up chemical reactions. Every living cell contains hundreds of enzymes that help the processes of life continue.

ester: organic compounds formed by the reaction of an alcohol with an acid and which often have a fruity taste. *Example:* ethyl acetate ($CH_3COOC_2H_5$).

evaporation: the change of state of a liquid to a gas. Evaporation happens below the boiling point and is used as a method of separating the materials in a solution.

excess, to: if a reactant has been added to another reactant in excess, it has exceeded the amount required to complete the reaction.

exothermic reaction: a reaction that gives out substantial amounts of heat. *Example:* sucrose and concentrated sulfuric acid.

explosive: a substance that, when a shock is applied to it, decomposes very rapidly, releasing a very large amount of heat and creating a large volume of gases as a shock wave.

fat: semisolid, energy-rich compounds derived from plants or animals, made of carbon, hydrogen, and oxygen.

ferment: to break down a substance by microorganisms in the absence of oxygen. *Example:* fermentation of sugar to ethyl alcohol during the production of alcoholic drinks.

filtrate: the liquid that has passed through a filter.

filtration: the separation of a liquid from a solid using a membrane with small holes (i.e. a filter paper).

flame: a mixture of gases undergoing burning. A solid or liquid must produce a gas before it can react with oxygen and burn with a flame.

flammable (also inflammable): able to burn (in air). *Opposite:* nonflammable.

flocculation: the grouping together of small particles in a suspension to form particles large enough to settle out as a precipitate. Flocculation is usually caused by the presence of a flocculating agent. *Example:* calcium ions are the flocculating agent for suspended clay particles.

fluid: able to flow; either a liquid or a gas.

fluorescent: a substance that gives out visible light when struck by invisible waves, such as ultraviolet rays.

flux: a material used to make it easier for a liquid to flow. A flux dissolves metal oxides and so prevents a metal from oxidizing while being heated.

foam: a substance that is sufficiently gelatinous to be able to contain bubbles of gas. The gas bulks up the substance, making it behave as though it were semirigid.

fossil fuels: hydrocarbon compounds that have been formed from buried plant and animal remains. High pressures and temperatures lasting over millions of years are required. *Examples:* The fossil fuels are coal, oil and natural gas.

fraction: a group of similar components of a mixture. *Example:* In the petroleum industry the light fractions of crude oil are those with the smallest molecules, while the medium and heavy fractions have larger molecules.

fractional distillation: the separation of the components of a liquid mixture by heating them to their boiling points.

fractionating column: a glass column designed to allow different fractions to be separated when they boil. In industry it may be called a fractionating tower.

free radical: a very reactive atom or group with a "spare" electron. *Example:* methyl, $CH_3\bullet$.

freezing point: the temperature at which a substance undergoes a phase change from a liquid to a solid. It is the same temperature as the melting point.

fuel: a concentrated form of chemical energy. The main sources of fuels (called fossil fuels because

they were formed by geological processes) are coal, crude oil, and natural gas.

fuel rods: the rods of uranium or other radioactive material used as a fuel in nuclear power plants.

fume chamber or fume cupboard: a special laboratory chamber fitted with a protective glass shield and containing a powerful extraction fan to remove toxic fumes.

fuming: an unstable liquid that gives off a gas. Very concentrated acid solutions are often fuming solutions. *Example:* fuming nitric acid.

galvanizing: applying a thin zinc coating to protect another metal.

gamma rays: waves of radiation produced as the nucleus of a radioactive element rearranges itself into a tighter cluster of protons and neutrons. Gamma rays carry enough energy to damage living cells.

gangue: the unwanted material in an ore.

gas/gaseous phase: a form of matter in which the molecules form no definite shape and are free to move about to uniformly fill any vessel they are put in. A gas can easily be compressed into a much smaller volume.

gas syringe: a glass syringe with a graduated cylinder designed to collect and measure small amounts of gases produced during an experiment.

gelatinous precipitate: a precipitate that has a jelly-like appearance. *Example:* iron (III) hydroxide. Because a gelatinous precipitate is mostly water, it is of a similar density to water and will float or lie suspended in the liquid. *See:* granular precipitate.

glass: a transparent silicate without any crystal growth. It has a glassy luster and breaks with a curved fracture. Note that some minerals have all these features and are therefore natural glasses. Household glass is a synthetic silicate.

glucose: the most common of the natural sugars ($C_6H_{12}O_6$). It occurs as the polymer known as cellulose, the fiber in plants. Starch is also a form of glucose.

granular precipitate: a precipitate that has a grainlike appearance. *Example:* lead(II) hydroxide. *See:* gelatinous precipitate.

gravimetric analysis: a quantitative form of analysis in which the mass (weight) of the reactants and products is measured.

group: a vertical column in the Periodic Table. There are eight groups in the table. Their numbers correspond to the number of electrons in the outer shell of the atoms in the group. *Example:* Group 1: member, sodium.

Greenhouse Effect: an increase in the global air temperature as a result of heat released from burning fossil fuels being absorbed by carbon dioxide in the atmosphere.

Greenhouse gas: any of various gases that contribute to the Greenhouse Effect. *Example:* carbon dioxide.

half-life: the time it takes for the radiation coming from a sample of a radioactive element to decrease by half.

halide: a salt of one of the halogens.

halogen: one of a group of elements including chlorine, bromine, iodine, and fluorine in Group 7 of the Periodic Table.

heat: the energy that is transferred when a substance is at a different temperature than its surroundings. *See:* endothermic and exothermic reactions.

heat capacity: the ratio of the heat supplied to a substance compared to the rise in temperature that is produced.

heat of combustion: the amount of heat given off by a mole of a substance during combustion. This heat is a property of the substance and is the same no matter what kind of combustion is involved. *Example:* heat of combustion of carbon is 94.05 kcal (✗ 4.18 = 393.1 kJ).

hydrate: a solid compound in crystalline form that contains water molecules. Hydrates commonly form when a solution of a soluble salt is evaporated. The water that forms part of a hydrate crystal is known as the "water of crystallization." It can usually be removed by heating, leaving an anhydrous salt.

hydration: the process of absorption of water by a substance. In some cases hydration makes the substance change color; in many other cases there is no color change, simply a change in volume. *Example:* dark blue hydrated copper(II) sulfate ($CuSO_4 \cdot 5H_2O$) can be heated to produce white anhydrous copper(II) sulfate ($CuSO_4$).

hydride: a compound containing just hydrogen and another element, most often a metal. *Examples:* water (H_2O), methane (CH_4) and phosphine (PH_3).

hydrous: hydrated with water. *See:* anhydrous.

hydrocarbon: a compound in which only hydrogen and carbon atoms are present. Most fuels are hydrocarbons, as is the simple plastic polyethylene. *Example:* methane CH_4.

hydrogen bond: a type of attractive force that holds one molecule to another. It is one of the weaker forms of intermolecular attractive force. *Example:* hydrogen bonds occur in water.

ignition temperature: the temperature at which a substance begins to burn.

immiscible: will not mix with another substance. e.g., oil and water.

incandescent: glowing or shining with heat. *Example:* tungsten filament in an incandescent light bulb.

incomplete combustion: combustion in which only some of the reactant or reactants combust, or the products are not those that would be obtained if all the reactions went to completion. It is uncommon for combustion to be complete, and incomplete combustion is more frequent. *Example:* incomplete combustion of carbon in oxygen produces carbon monoxide and not carbon dioxide.

indicator (acid-base indicator): a substance or mixture of substances used to test the acidity or alkalinity of a substance. An indicator changes color depending on the acidity of the solution being tested. Many indicators are complicated organic substances. Some indicators used in the laboratory include Universal Indicator, litmus, phenolphthalein, methyl orange and bromothymol. *See:* Universal Indicator.

induction period: the time taken for a reaction to reach ignition temperature. During this period no apparent reaction occurs; then the materials appear to undergo spontaneous combustion.

inert: unreactive.

inhibitor: a substance that prevents a reaction from occurring.

inorganic substance: a substance that does not contain carbon and hydrogen. Examples: $NaCl$, $CaCO_3$.

insoluble: a substance that will not dissolve.

ion: an atom, or group of atoms, that has gained or lost one or more electrons and so developed an electrical charge. Ions behave differently than electrically neutral atoms and molecules. They can move in an electric field, and they can also bind strongly to solvent molecules such as water. Positively charged ions are called cations; negatively charged ions are called anions. Ions can carry an electrical current through solutions.

ionic bond: the form of bonding that occurs between two ions when the ions have opposite charges. *Example:* sodium cations bond with chloride anions to form common salt ($NaCl$) when a salty solution is evaporated. Ionic bonds are strong bonds except in the presence of a solvent. *See:* bond.

ionic compound: a compound that consists of ions. *Example:* $NaCl$.

ionize: to break up neutral molecules into oppositely charged ions or to convert atoms into ions by the loss of electrons.

ionization: a process that creates ions.

isotope: an atom that has the same number of protons in its nucleus, but which has a different mass. *Example:* carbon 12 and carbon 14.

Kipp's apparatus: a piece of glassware consisting of three chambers, designed to provide a continuous and regulated production of gas by bringing the reactants into contact in a controlled way.

lanthanide series or lanthanide metals: a series of 15 similar metallic elements between lanthanum and lutetium. They are transition metals and are also called rare earths.

latent heat: the amount of heat that is absorbed or released during the process of changing state between gas, liquid, or solid. For example, heat is absorbed when a substance melts, and it is released again when the substance solidifies.

lattice: a regular arrangement of atoms, ions, or molecules in a crystalline solid.

leaching: the extraction of a substance by percolating a solvent through a material. *Example:* when water flows through an ore, some of the heavy metals in it may be leached out causing environmental pollution.

Liebig condenser: a piece of glassware consisting of a sloping, water-cooled tube. The design allows a volatile material to be condensed and collected.

liquefaction: to make something liquid.

liquid/liquid phase: a form of matter that has a fixed volume but no fixed shape.

lime (quicklime): calcium oxide (CaO). A white, caustic solid manufactured by heating limestone and used for making mortar, fertilizer, or bleach.

limewater: an aqueous solution of calcium hydroxide used especially to detect the presence of carbon dioxide.

litmus: an indicator obtained from lichens. Used as a solution or impregnated into paper (litmus paper) that is dampened before use. Litmus turns red under acid conditions and purple in alkaline conditions. Litmus is a crude indicator when compared with Universal Indicator.

load (electronics): an impedance or circuit that receives or develops the output of a cell or other power supply.

luster: the shininess of a substance.

malleable: able to be pressed or hammered into shape.

manometer: a device for measuring gas pressure. A simple manometer is made by partly filling a U-shaped rubber tube with water and connecting one end to the source of gas whose pressure is to be measured. The pressure is always relative to atmospheric pressure.

mass: the amount of matter in an object. In everyday use the word weight is often used (somewhat incorrectly) to mean mass.

matter: anything that has mass and takes up space.

melting point: the temperature at which a substance changes state from a solid phase to a liquid phase. It is the same as freezing point.

membrane: a thin flexible sheet. A semipermeable membrane has microscopic holes of a size that will selectively allow some ions and molecules to pass through but hold others back. It thus acts as a kind of filter. *Example:* a membrane used for osmosis.

meniscus: the curved surface of a liquid that forms in a small-bore or capillary tube. The meniscus is convex (bulges upward) for mercury and is concave (sags downward) for water.

metal: a class of elements that is a good conductor of electricity and heat, has a metallic luster, is malleable and ductile, forms cations, and has oxides that are bases. Metals are formed as cations held together by a sea of electrons. A metal may also be an alloy of these elements. *Example:* sodium, calcium, gold. *See:* alloy, metalloid, nonmetal.

metallic bonding: cations reside in a "sea" of mobile electrons. It allows metals to be good conductors and means that they are not brittle. *See:* bonding.

metallic luster: *See:* luster.

metalloid: a class of elements intermediate in properties between metals and nonmetals. Metalloids are also called semimetals or semiconductors. *Example:* silicon, germanium, antimony. *See:* metal, nonmetal, semiconductor.

micronutrient: an element that the body requires in small amounts. Another term is trace element.

mineral: a solid substance made of just one element or compound. *Example:* calcite is a mineral because it consists only of calcium carbonate; halite is a mineral because it contains only sodium chloride.

mineral acid: an acid that does not contain carbon and which attacks minerals. Hydrochloric, sulfuric, and nitric acids are the main mineral acids.

miscible: capable of being mixed.

mixing combustion: the form of combustion that occurs when two gases thoroughly mix before they ignite and so produce almost complete combustion. *Example:* when a Bunsen flame is blue.

mixture: a material that can be separated into two or more substances using physical means. *Example:* a mixture of copper(II) sulfate and cadmium sulfide can be separated by filtration.

molar mass: the mass per mole of atoms of an element. It has the same value and uses the same units as atomic weight. *Example:* molar mass of chlorine is 35.45 g/mol. *See:* atomic weight.

mole: 1 mole is the amount of a substance that contains Avagadro's number (6×10^{23}) of particles. *Example:* 1 mole of carbon-12 weighs exactly 12 g.

molecular mass: *See:* molar mass.

molecular weight: *See:* molar mass.

molecule: a group of two or more atoms held together by chemical bonds. *Example:* 0_2.

monoclinic system: a grouping of crystals that look like double-ended chisel blades.

monomer: a small molecule and building block for larger chain molecules or polymers ("mono"

means one, "mer" means part). *Examples:* tetrafluoroethene for teflon, ethene for polyethene.

native element: an element that occurs in an uncombined state. *Examples:* sulfur, gold.

native metal: a pure form of a metal, not combined as a compound. Native metal is more common in poorly reactive elements than in those that are very reactive. *Examples:* copper, gold.

net ionic reaction: the overall, or net, change that occurs in a reaction, seen in terms of ions.

neutralization: the reaction of acids and bases to produce a salt and water. The reaction causes hydrogen from the acid and hydroxide from the base to be changed to water. *Example:* hydrochloric acid reacts with, and neutralizes, sodium hydroxide to form the salt sodium chloride (common salt) and water. The term is more generally used for any reaction in which the pH changes toward 7.0, which is the pH of a neutral solution. *See:* pH.

neutralization point: *See:* end point.

neutron: a particle inside the nucleus of an atom that is neutral and has no charge.

newton (N): the unit of force required to give one kilogram an acceleration of one meter per second every second (1 ms⁻²).

nitrate: a compound that includes nitrogen and oxygen and contains more oxygen than a nitrite. Nitrate ions have the chemical formula NO_3^-. *Examples:* sodium nitrate $NaNO_3$ and lead nitrate $Pb(NO_3)_2$.

nitrite: a compound that includes nitrogen and oxygen and contains less oxygen than a nitrate. Nitrite ions have the chemical formula NO_2^-. *Example:* sodium nitrite $NaNO_2$.

noble gases: the members of Group 8 of the Periodic Table: helium, neon, argon, krypton, xenon, radon. These gases are almost entirely unreactive.

noble metals: silver, gold, platinum, and mercury. These are the least reactive metals.

noncombustible: a substance that will not combust or burn. *Example:* carbon dioxide.

nonmetal: a brittle substance that does not conduct electricity. *Examples:* sulfur, phosphorus, all gases. *See:* metal, metalloid.

normal salt: salts that do not contain a hydroxide (OH^-) ion, which would make them basic salts, or a hydrogen ion, which would make them acid salts. *Example:* sodium chloride (NaCl).

nucleus: the small, positively charged particle at the center of an atom. The nucleus is responsible for most of the mass of an atom.

opaque: a substance that will not transmit light so that it is impossible to see through it. Most solids are opaque.

ore: a rock containing enough of a useful substance to make mining it worthwhile. *Example:* bauxite, aluminum ore.

organic acid: an acid containing carbon and hydrogen. *Example:* methanoic (formic) acid (HCOOH).

organic chemistry: the study of organic compounds.

organic compound (organic substance; organic material): a compound (or substance) that contains carbon and usually hydrogen. (The carbonates are usually excluded.) *Examples:* methane (CH_4), chloromethane (CH_3Cl), ethene (C_2H_4), ethanol (C_2H_5OH), ethanoic acid (C_2H_3OOH) etc.

organic solvent: an organic substance that will dissolve other substances. *Example:* carbon tetrachloride (CCl_4).

osmosis: a process whereby molecules of a liquid solvent move through a semipermeable membrane from a region of low concentration of a solute to a region with a high concentration of a solute.

oxidation-reduction reaction (redox reaction): reaction in which oxidation and reduction occurs; a reaction in which electrons are transferred. *Example:* copper and oxygen react to produce copper(II) oxide. The copper is oxidized, and oxygen is reduced.

oxidation: combination with oxygen or a reaction in which an atom, ion, or molecule loses electrons to an oxidizing agent. (Note that an oxidizing agent does not have to contain oxygen.) The opposite of oxidation is reduction. *See:* reduction.

oxidation number (oxidation state): the effective charge on an atom in a compound. An increase in oxidation number corresponds to oxidation, and a decrease to reduction. Shown in Roman numerals. *Example:* manganate(IV).

oxidation state: *See:* oxidation number.

oxide: a compound that includes oxygen and one other element. *Example:* copper oxide (CuO).

oxidize: to combine with or gain oxygen or to react such that an atom, ion, or molecule loses electrons to an oxidizing agent.

oxidizing agent: a substance that removes electrons from another substance being oxidized (and therefore is itself reduced) in a redox reaction. *Example:* chlorine (Cl_2).

ozone: a form of oxygen whose molecules contain three atoms of oxygen. Ozone is regarded as a beneficial gas when high in the atmosphere because it blocks ultraviolet rays. It is a harmful gas when breathed in, so low-level ozone that is produced as part of city smog is regarded as a form of pollution. The ozone layer is the uppermost part of the stratosphere.

partial pressure: the pressure a gas in a mixture would exert if it alone occupied a flask. *Example:* oxygen makes up about a fifth of the atmosphere. Its partial pressure is therefore about a fifth of normal atmospheric pressure.

pascal: the unit of pressure, equal to one newton per square meter of surface. *See:* newton.

patina: a surface coating that develops on metals and protects them from further corrosion. *Example:* the green coating on copper carbonate that forms on copper statues.

percolate: to move slowly through the pores of a rock.

period: a row in the Periodic Table.

Periodic Table: a chart organizing elements by atomic number and chemical properties into groups and periods.

pestle and mortar: a pestle is a ceramic rod with a rounded end; a mortar is a ceramic dish. Pestle and mortar are used together to pound or grind solids into fine powders.

Petri dish: a shallow glass or plastic dish with a lid.

petroleum: a natural mixture of a range of gases, liquids, and solids derived from the decomposed remains of plants and animals.

pH: a measure of the hydrogen ion concentration in a liquid. Neutral is pH 7.0; numbers greater than this are alkaline; smaller numbers are acidic. *See:* neutralization, acid, base.

pH meter: a device that accurately measures the pH of a solution. A

pH meter is a voltmeter that measures the electric potential difference between two electrodes (which are attached to the meter through a probe) when they are submerged in a solution. The readings are shown on a dial or digital display.

phase: a particular state of matter. A substance may exist as a solid, liquid, or gas and may change between these phases with addition or removal of energy. *Examples:* ice, liquid, and vapor are the three phases of water. Ice undergoes a phase change to water when heat energy is added.

phosphor: any material that glows when energized by ultraviolet or electron beams such as in fluorescent tubes and cathode ray tubes. Phosphors, such as phosphorus, emit light after the source of excitation is cut off. This is why they glow in the dark. By contrast, fluorescors, such as fluorite, only emit light while they are being excited by ultraviolet light or an electron beam.

photochemical smog: photochemical reactions are caused by the energy of sunlight. Photochemical smog is a mixture of tiny particles and a brown haze caused by the reaction of colorless nitric oxide from vehicle exhausts and oxygen of the air to form brown nitrogen dioxide.

photon: a parcel of light energy.

photosynthesis: the process by which plants use the energy of the Sun to make the compounds they need for life. In photosynthesis six molecules of carbon dioxide from the air combine with six molecules of water, forming one molecule of glucose (sugar) and releasing six molecules of oxygen back into the atmosphere.

pipe-clay triangle: a device made from three small pieces of ceramic tube that are wired together in the shape of a triangle. Pipe-clay

triangles are used to support round-bottomed dishes when they are heated in a Bunsen flame.

pipette: a log, slender glass tube used, in conjunction with a pipette filler, to draw up and then transfer accurately measured amounts of liquid.

plastic: (material) a carbon-based substance consisting of long chains (polymers) of simple molecules. The word plastic is commonly restricted to synthetic polymers. *Examples:* polyvinyl chloride, nylon: **(property)** a material is plastic if it can be made to change shape easily. Plastic materials will remain in the new shape. (Compare with elastic, a property whereby a material goes back to its original shape.)

pneumatic trough: a shallow water-filled glass dish used to house a beehive shelf and a gas jar as part of the apparatus for collecting a gas over water.

polar solvent: a solvent in which the atoms have partial electric charges. *Example:* water.

polymer: a compound that is made of long chains by combining molecules (called monomers) as repeating units. ("Poly" means many, "mer" means part.) *Examples:* polytetrafluoroethene or Teflon from tetrafluoroethene, Terylene from terephthalic acid and ethane-1,2-diol (ethylene glycol).

polymerization: a chemical reaction in which large numbers of similar molecules arrange themselves into large molecules, usually long chains. This process usually happens when there is a suitable catalyst present. *Example:* ethene gas reacts to form polyethene in the presence of certain catalysts.

polymorphism: (meaning many shapes) the tendency of some materials to have more than one solid form. *Example:* carbon as diamond, graphite and buckminsterfullerene.

porous: a material containing many small holes or cracks. Quite often the pores are connected, and liquids, such as water or oil, can move through them.

potential difference: a measure of the work that must be done to move an electric charge from one point to the other in a circuit. Potential difference is measured in volts, V. *See:* electrical potential.

precious metal: silver, gold, platinum, iridium and palladium. Each is prized for its rarity.

precipitate: a solid substance formed as a result of a chemical reaction between two liquids or gases. *Example:* iron (III) hydroxide is precipitated when sodium hydroxide solution is added to iron (III) chloride. *See:* gelatinous precipitate, granular precipitate.

preservative: a substance that prevents the natural organic decay processes from occurring. Many substances can be used safely for this purpose, including sulfites and nitrogen gas.

pressure: the force per unit area measured in pascals. *See:* pascal.

product: a substance produced by a chemical reaction. *Example:* when the reactants copper and oxygen react, they produce the product copper oxide.

proton: a positively charged particle in the nucleus of an atom that balances out the charge of the surrounding electrons.

proton number: this is the modern expression for atomic number. *See:* atomic number.

purify: to remove all impurities from a mixture, perhaps by precipitation or filtration.

pyrolysis: chemical decomposition brought about by heat. *Example:* decomposition of lead nitrate. *See:* destructive distillation.

pyrometallurgy: refining a metal from its ore using heat. A blast furnace or smelter is the main equipment used.

quantitative: measurement of the amounts of constituents of a substance, for example, by mass or volume. *See:* gravimetric analysis, volumetric analysis.

radiation: the exchange of energy with the surroundings through the transmission of waves or particles of energy. Radiation is a form of energy transfer that can happen through space; no intervening medium is required (as would be the case for conduction and convection).

radical: an atom, molecule, or ion with at least one unpaired electron. *Example:* nitrogen monoxide (NO).

radioactive: emitting radiation or particles from the nucleus of its atoms.

radioactive decay: a change in a radioactive element due to loss of mass through radiation. For example, uranium decays (changes) to lead.

reactant: a starting material that takes part in and undergoes change during a chemical reaction. *Example:* hydrochloric acid and calcium carbonate are reactants; the reaction produces the products calcium chloride, carbon dioxide, and water.

reaction: the recombination of two substances using parts of each substance to produce new substances. *Example:* the reactants sodium chloride and sulfuric acid react and recombine to form the products sodium sulfate, chlorine, and water.

reactivity: the tendency of a substance to react with other substances. The term is most widely used in comparing the reactivity of metals. Metals are arranged in a reactivity series.

reactivity series: the series of metals organized in order of their reactivity, with the most reactive metals, such as sodium, at the top and the least react metals, such as gold, at the bottom. Hydrogen is usually included in the series for comparative purposes.

reagent: a commonly available substance (reactant) used to create a reaction. Reagents are the chemicals normally kept on chemistry laboratory shelf. Many substances called reagents are most commonly used for test purposes.

redox reaction (oxidation-reduction reaction): a reaction that involves oxidation and reduction; a reactions in which electrons are transferred. *See:* oxidation-reduction.

reducing agent: a substance that gives electrons to another substance being reduced (and therefore itself being oxidized) in a redox reaction. *Example:* hydrogen sulfide (H_2S).

reduction: the removal of oxygen from, or the addition of hydrogen to, a compound. Also a reaction in which an atom, ion, or molecule gains electrons from an reducing agent. (The opposite of reduction is oxidation.)

reduction tube: a boiling tube with a small hole near the closed end. The tube is mounted horizontally, a sample is placed in the tube, and a reducing gas, such as carbon monoxide, is passed through the tube. The oxidized gas escapes through the small hole.

refining: separating a mixture into the simpler substances of which it is made.

reflux distillation system: a form of distillation using a Liebig condenser placed vertically, so that all the vapors created during boiling are condensed back into the liquid rather than escaping. In this way the concentration of all the reactants remains constant.

relative atomic mass: in the past a measure of the mass of an atom on a scale relative to the mass of an atom of hydrogen, where hydrogen is 1. Nowadays a measure of the mass of an atom relative to the mass of one twelfth of an atom of carbon-12. If the relative atomic mass is given as a rounded figure, it is called an approximate relative atomic mass. *Examples*: chlorine 35, calcium 40, gold 197. *See:* atomic mass, atomic weight.

reversible reaction: a reaction in which the products can be transformed back into their original chemical form. *Example:* heated iron reacts with steam to produce iron oxide and hydrogen. If the hydrogen is passed over this heated oxide it forms iron and steam. $3Fe + 4H_2O \rightleftharpoons Fe_3O_4 + 4H_2$.

roast: heating a substance for a long time at a high temperature, as in a furnace.

rust: the product of the corrosion of iron and steel in the presence of air and water.

salt: a compound, often involving a metal, that is the reaction product of an acid and a base, or of two elements. (Note "salt" is also the common word for sodium chloride, common salt, or table salt.) *Example:* sodium chloride ($NaCl$) and potassium sulfate (K_2SO_4) *See:* acid salt, basic salt, normal salt.

salt bridge: a permeable material soaked in a salt solution that allows ions to be transferred from one container to another. The salt solution remains unchanged during this transfer. *Example:* sodium sulfate used as a salt bridge in a galvanic cell.

saponification: a reaction between a fat and a base that produces a soap.

saturated: a state in which a liquid can hold no more of a substance. If any more of the substance is added, it will not dissolve.

saturated hydrocarbon: a hydrocarbon in which the carbon atoms are held with single bonds. *Example:* ethane (C_2H_4).

saturated solution: a solution that holds the maximum possible amount of dissolved material. When saturated, the rate of dissolving solid and that of recrystallization solid are the same, and a condition of equilibrium is reached. The amount of material in solution varies with the temperature; cold solutions can hold less dissolved solid material than hot solutions. Gases are more soluble in cold liquids than hot liquids.

sediment: material that settles out at the bottom of a liquid when it is still. A precipitate is one form of sediment.

semiconductor: a material of intermediate conductivity. Semiconductor devices often use silicon when they are made as part of diodes, transistors, or integrated circuits. Elements intermediate between metals and nonmetals are also sometimes called semiconductors. *Example:* germanium oxide, germanium. *See:* metalloid.

semipermeable membrane: a thin material that acts as a fine sieve or filter, allowing small molecules to pass, but holding large molecules back.

separating column: used in chromatography. A tall glass tube containing a porous disc near the base and filled with a substance (for example, aluminum oxide, which is known as a stationary phase) that can adsorb materials on its surface. When a mixture is passed through the column, fractions are retarded by differing amounts, so that each fraction is washed through the column in sequence.

separating funnel: a pear-shaped glassware funnel designed to permit the separation of immiscible liquids by simply pouring off the more dense liquid while leaving the less dense liquid in the funnel.

series circuit: an electrical circuit in which all of the components are joined end to end in a line.

shell: the term used to describe the imaginary ball-shaped surface outside the nucleus of an atom that would be formed by a set of electrons of similar energy. The outermost shell is known as the valence shell. *Example:* neon has shells containing 2 and 8 electrons.

side-arm boiling tube: a boiling tube with an integral glass pipe near its open end. The side arm is normally used for the entry or exit of a gas.

simple distillation: the distillation of a substance when only one volatile fraction is to be collected. Simple distillation uses a Liebig condenser arranged almost horizontally. When the liquid mixture is heated and vapors are produced, they enter the condenser and then flow away from the flask and can be collected. *Example:* simple distillation of ethanoic acid.

slag: a mixture of substances that are waste products of a furnace. Most slags are composed mainly of silicates.

smelting: roasting a substance in order to extract the metal contained in it.

smog: a mixture of smoke and fog. The term is used to describe city fogs in which there is a large proportion of particulate matter (tiny pieces of carbon from exhausts) and also a high concentration of sulfur and nitrogen gases and probably ozone. *See:* photochemical smog.

smokeless fuel: a fuel that has been subjected to partial pyrolysis so that there is no more loose particulate matter remaining. *Example:* Coke is a smokeless fuel.

solid/solid phase: a rigid form of matter that maintains its shape whatever its container.

solubility: the maximum amount of a substance that can be contained in a solvent.

soluble: readily dissolvable in a solvent.

solute: a substance that has dissolved. *Example:* sodium chloride in water.

solution: a mixture of a liquid (the solvent) and at least one other substance of lesser abundance (the solute). Mixtures can be separated by physical means, for example, by evaporation and cooling. *See:* aqueous solution.

solvent: the main substance in a solution.

spectator ions: the ionic part of a compound that does not play an active part in a reaction. *Example:* when magnesium ribbon is placed in copper(II) sulfate solution the copper is displaced from the solution by the magnesium while the sulfate ion (SO_4^{2-}) plays no part in the reaction and so behaves as a spectator ion.

spectrum: the range of colors that make up visible light (as seen in a rainbow) or across all electromagnetic radiation, arranged in progression according to their wavelength.

spontaneous combustion: the effect of a very reactive material or combination of reactants that suddenly reach their ignition temperature and begin to combust rapidly.

standard temperature and pressure (STP): 0°C at one atmosphere (a pressure that supports a column of mercury 760 mm high). Also given as 0°C at 100 kilopascals. *See:* atmospheric pressure.

state of matter: the physical form of matter. There are three states of matter: liquid, solid, and gaseous.

stationary phase: a name given to a material that is used as a medium for separating a liquid mixture, as in in chromatography.

strong acid: an acid that has completely dissociated (ionized) in water. Mineral acids are strong acids.

sublime/sublimation: the change of a substance from solid to gas, or vice versa, without going through a liquid phase. *Example:* iodine sublimes from a purple solid to a purple gas.

substance: a type of material, including mixtures.

sulfate: a compound that includes sulfur and oxygen and contains more oxygen than a sulfite. Sulfate ions have the chemical formula SO_4^{2-}. *Examples:* calcium sulfate $CaSO_4$ (the main constituent of gypsum) and aluminum sulfate $Al_2(SO_4)_3$ (an alum).

sulfide: a sulfur compound that contains no oxygen. Sulfide ions have the chemical formula S^{2-}. *Example:* hydrogen sulfide (H_2S).

sulfite: a compound that includes sulfur and oxygen but contains less oxygen than a sulfate. Sulfite ions have the chemical formula SO_3^{2-}. *Example:* sodium sulfite Na_2SO_3.

supercooling: the ability of some substances to cool below their normal freezing point. *Example:* sodium thiosulfate.

supersaturated solution: a solution in which the amount of solute is greater than what would normally be expected in a saturated solution. Most solids are more soluble in hot solutions than in cold. If a hot saturated solution is made up, the solution can be rapidly cooled down below its freezing point before it begins to solidify. This is a supersaturated solution.

surface tension: the force that operates on the surface of a liquid and that makes it act as though it were covered with an invisible, elastic film.

suspension: a mist of tiny particles in a liquid.

synthesis: a reaction in which a substance is formed from simpler reactants. *Example:* hydrogen gas and chlorine gas react to sythesize hydrogen chloride gas. The term can also be applied to polymerization of organic compounds.

synthetic: does not occur naturally but has to be manufactured. Commonly used in the name "synthetic fiber."

tare: an allowance made for the weight of a container.

tarnish: a coating that develops as a result of the reaction between a metal and substances in the air. The most common form of tarnishing is a very thin transparent oxide coating.

terminal: one of the electrodes of a battery.

test (chemical): a reagent or a procedure used to reveal the presence of another reagent. *Example:* litmus and other indicators are used to test the acidity or alkalinity of a substance.

test tube: A thin glass tube closed at one end and used for chemical tests, etc. The composition and thickness of the glass is such that while it is inert to most chemical reactions, it may not sustain very high temperatures but can usually be heated in a Bunsen flame. *See:* boiling tube.

thermal decomposition: the breakdown of a substance using heat: *See* pyrolysis.

thermoplastic: a plastic that will soften and can repeatedly be molded into shape on heating and

will set into the molded shape as it cools.

thermoset: a plastic that will set into a molded shape as it cools, but which cannot be made soft by reheating.

thistle funnel: a narrow tube, expanded at the top into a thistlehead-shaped vessel. It is used as a funnel when introducing small amounts of liquid reactant. When fitted with a tap, it can be used to control the rate of entry of a reactant. *See:* burette.

titration: the analysis of the composition of a substance in a solution by measuring the volume of that solution (the titrant, normally in a burette) needed to react with a given volume of another solution (the titrate, normally placed in a flask). An indicator is often used to signal change. *Example:* neutralization of sodium hydroxide using hydrochloric acid in an acid–base titration. *See:* end point.

toxic: poisonous.

transition metals: the group of metals that belong to the d-block of the Periodic Table. Transition metals commonly have a number of differently colored oxidation states. *Examples:* iron, vanadium.

Universal Indicator: a mixture of indicators commonly used in the laboratory because of its reliability. Used as a solution or impregnated into paper (Indicator paper) that is dampened before use. Universal Indicator changes color from purple in a strongly alkaline solution through green when the solution is neutral to red in strongly acidic solutions. Universal Indicator is more accurate than litmus paper but less accurate than a pH meter.

unsaturated hydrocarbon: a hydrocarbon in which at least one bond is a double or triple bond. Hydrogen atoms can be added to

unsaturated compounds to form saturated compounds. *Example:* ethene, C_2H_4 or $CH_2=CH_2$.

vacuum: a container from which air has been removed using a pump.

valency: the number of bonds that an atom can form. *Examples:* calcium has a valency of 2 and bromine a valency of 1

valency shell: the outermost shell of an atom. *See:* shell.

vapor: the gaseous phase of a substance. *See:* gas.

vein: a fissure in rock that has filled with ore or other mineral-bearing rock.

viscous: slow-moving, syrupy. A liquid that has a low viscosity is said to be mobile.

volatile: readily forms a gas.

volatile fraction: the part of a liquid mixture that will readily vaporize under the conditions prevailing during the reaction. *See:* fraction, vapor.

water of crystallization: the water molecules absorbed into the crystalline structure as a liquid changes to a solid. *Example:* hydrated copper(II) sulfate $CuSO_4 \cdot 5H_2O$. *See:* hydrate.

weak acid and **weak base**: an acid or base that has only partly dissociated (ionized) in water. Most organic acids are weak acids. *See:* organic acid.

weight: the gravitational force on a substance. *See:* mass.

X-rays: a form of very short wave radiation.

MASTER INDEX

21.60

540 C
ChemLab.
Heat and combustion. V. 6.